# DAY TRIPS®
## FROM SACRAMENTO

"Hooray for *Day Trips from Sacramento*! . . . Fun to read and like advice from a good friend, [it] will steer you the right way to maximize your vacation dollar."

—Arthur von Wiesenberger, *Around the World with Arthur & Barney*, KEYT Newsradio 1250

## Help Us Keep This Guide Up to Date

Every effort has been made by the author and editors to make this guide as accurate and useful as possible. Many things, however, can change after a guide is published—establishments close, phone numbers change, facilities come under new management, etc.

We would love to hear from you concerning your experiences with this guide and how you feel it could be made better and be kept up to date. While we may not be able to respond to all comments and suggestions, we'll take them to heart and we'll make certain to share them with the author. Please send your comments and suggestions to the following address:

The Globe Pequot Press
Reader Response/Editorial Department
P.O. Box 480
Guilford, CT 06437

Or you may e-mail us at:
editorial@globe-pequot.com

Thanks for your input, and happy travels!

*Day Trips® Series*

**GETAWAYS LESS THAN TWO HOURS AWAY**

# DAY TRIPS®
# FROM SACRAMENTO

*by*
**Stephen Metzger**

The Globe Pequot Press

GUILFORD, CONNECTICUT

Copyright © 2000 by The Globe Pequot Press

Cover image: Chris Dubé Studio
Maps: William L. Nelson and M.A. Dubé

Day Trips is a registered trademark of The Globe Pequot Press.

**Library of Congress Cataloging-in-Publication Data**
Metzger, Stephen, 1954-
    Day Trips from Sacramento : getaways less than two hours away/
by Stephen Metzger. — 1st ed.
    p. cm. — (Day trips series)
ISBN 0-7627-0717-8
    1. Sacramento Region (Calif.) — Guidebooks.  I.  Title: Day trips from Sacramento.  II. Title.  III. Series.

F869.S12 M48 2000
917.94'540453—dc21                      00-037637

Manufactured in the United States of America
First Edition/First Printing

**To Betz,
my wife and best friend**

# CONTENTS

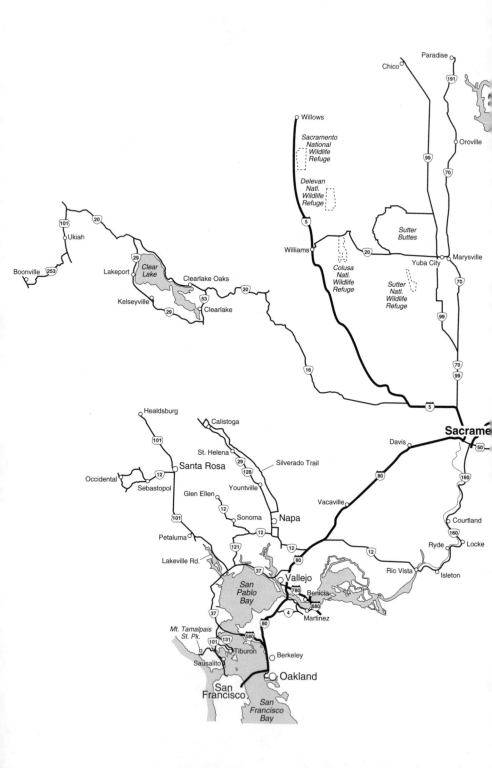

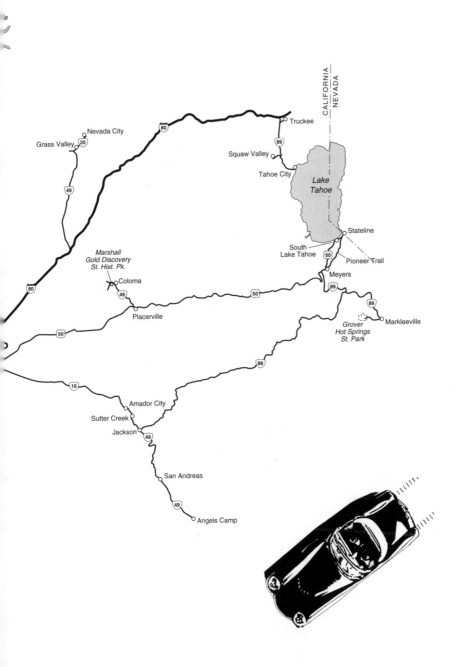

Nevada City

Grass Valley

Truckee

CALIFORNIA
NEVADA

Squaw Valley

Tahoe City

Lake
Tahoe

Stateline

South
Lake Tahoe

Pioneer Trail

Marshall
Gold Discovery
St. Hist. Pk.

Coloma

Meyers

Placerville

Grover
Hot Springs
St. Park

Markleeville

Amador City

Sutter Creek

Jackson

San Andreas

Angels Camp

# ACKNOWLEDGMENTS

A lot of good people helped me with this book, and I'm grateful to all of them. First of all, Kim Weir suggested to the publisher that I might be the right person for this job. I'm also thankful to three of my former students whose knowledge of their hometowns, coupled with their graceful and insightful writing, provided a credibility and legitimacy to the project that I wouldn't have been able to: Elyzabeth Hiscox got the inside scoop on Grass Valley and Nevada City; Erin Sierchio showed what makes Davis such an unusual and attractive destination; and Janet Greene got the lowdown on Yuba City and Marysville.

I'm also grateful to two old friends and fellow gourmands for their expert opinions and insights on Bay Area restaurants: Jeff Ray in Petaluma and Alix Schwartz in Berkeley. Also to my parents, not only for their support—as always—but also for their suggestions for wine country attractions.

Finally, to my family: I can't tell you how much your love and support means to me. And, Gina, thanks for the great research trip to the gold country. We'll take Hannah and Mom back to Mel's Diner.

# PREFACE

It would be difficult to think of a better place than Sacramento to be located for day trips. Situated in the center of the northern third of the state, Sacramento provides easy access to a huge range of scenery, geography, history, and activities, all under two hours away.

You can head west to the wine-growing regions of the Napa, Sonoma, and Anderson valleys, famous not only for their vineyards and wineries but for their excellent restaurants. You can go east to Lake Tahoe, where you'll find world-class snow skiing and some of the most stunning scenery on the planet. You can head southeast to the gold country, where the little gold-rush towns of Jackson, Sutter Creek, and Angels Camp are defined by historic hotels, gorgeous Victorian homes that cling to cliffsides, and museums that display the area's fascinating history. You can also head north, up into the Sacramento Valley, where wildlife refuges provide opportunities to view great flocks of migrating swans and snow geese and where the little university town of Chico offers a culture unlike any other in the valley, as well as the third-largest municipal park in the country. You can even head to the San Francisco Bay Area, to Oakland, Berkeley, Marin County, or San Francisco itself. Here you'll find nationally acclaimed restaurants, musems, shopping, and a mind-boggling diversity of ethnicities, cuisines, and lifestyles.

Keep in mind that the day trips I've suggested are just that, suggestions, and that all of them can be fine-tuned. For example, you couldn't possibly do in a day everything in San Francisco I've listed. That might take weeks. Better to pick and choose if it's truly a day trip you have in mind. On the other hand, you might want to combine some of the day trips I've listed. You could, for example, head northeast to Nevada City (Northeast Day Trip 1) and then go west from there to Marysville and Yuba City (North Day Trip 1). You could also go northeast to Truckee and North Lake Tahoe (Northeast Day Trip 2) and then head south to South Lake Tahoe (East Day Trip 2), returning to Sacramento from there. You could even go southwest to

San Francisco (Southwest Day Trip 3), then head across the Golden Gate Bridge, drive through Marin County (Southwest Day Trip 4), and drive home through Petaluma (West Day Trip 3).

Remember, too, that at most of the destinations I've included, you'll find lots more to do and see than I've been able to list. One could easily write an entire book about almost every single destination I've included. And that's why I always recommend beginning your trips at visitor-information centers, usually those sponsored by the chamber of commerce or a convention-and-visitors bureau. These places are packed with information on things to do and see in the area, as well as on local events, shopping, lodging, and dining (often they even have exhaustive collections of menus from nearby restaurants). Additionally, the visitor centers are staffed by friendly locals who are delighted to point out places of interest and to suggest things to do.

You'll find that most of the people you run into in your travels are quite friendly. Demonsrate an interest in their area by asking lots of questions, and you'll be making friends right and left. I've found one of the best ways to get to know locals is, whenever possible, to sit at the bar or counter of a restaurant. Obviously, this proabably doesn't make sense if you're traveling with a group of three or more, but if you're by yourself, or with one other person, grab a stool at the counter. It's more than likely that the guy sitting next to you—who has been working at the local lumbermill and fishing the nearby lakes for thirty years—will strike up a conversation. Plus, it's easier to ask questions of your waitress when she's wiping down the counter and waiting for her order to come up than when she's darting between tables, a tray held above her shoulder. You'll find that the waitstaff is often friendlier to folks sitting at the counter, perhaps assuming they're local themselves, than to those at tables.

*One last piece of advice:* Be respectful. Remember that folks live in these places you're visiting, and though they often rely on tourist dollars to keep the local economy afloat, they also are human's who deserve respect. Pay attention to local customs. Don't be loud. Don't litter. Say "Please" and "Thank you." Smile at people you don't know.

So head on out. Keep your eyes and mind open, and have a good time.

# TRAVEL TIPS

## Driving

You'll encounter just about every type of road imaginable as you venture out on day trips from Sacramento, from narrow country backroads to congested city streets, from wide, flat interstates to winding mountain passes. Generally, California roads are exceptionally well built, and CalTrans makes every effort to maintain them. Still, keeping a few things in mind will ensure your trip is that much safer.

First of all, make sure your car is in good shape. Don't head out with the "Check Oil" light on, and make sure your lights, windshield wipers, etc., are in good working order. Also, be sure to pack water and snacks, and if you can, bring along a cell phone, should you run into trouble of any kind.

Winter driving in the mountains can be especially tricky, as snow drifts across roadways, making visibility difficult, and even when the roads are dry, extreme caution must be taken. When the roads get snowy and wet, they're even more dangerous—chains and/or four-wheel-drive are often required—and drivers without experience in the snow should consider waiting until the routes have been cleared. Snowplows usually begin clearing major Sierra arteries as soon as the snow begins to pile up, and these routes are rarely closed very long. Lesser-traveled routes, lower on the priority list, take longer to get cleared.

In spring melted snow from warm daytime temperatures often trickles across roadways, and during the night this water freezes, resulting in hard-to-see sheets of ice on the road. These spots are even more slick and dangerous than patches of snow.

Here are some guidelines for driving in California mountains in winter:

- Pay attention to highway rules and regulations, including closures and chain requirements; they're meant for your safety.

- Make sure your brakes are in good working order and that your tires have plenty of tread.
- Make sure your cooling system has been properly winterized.
- Check your windshield wipers and wiper fluid; wiper fluid with antifreeze is available at auto-parts stores and gas stations.
- Always carry chains (assistants at chain-control spots can put them on for you, usually for a charge of about $20).
- Drive slowly, and always stay in control; remember that your car's stopping distance is greater when the road is wet, snowy, and/or icy.
- Stop if you begin to lose control or confidence.
- Keep seat belts fastened at all times (common sense as well as California state law).

For current road conditions, including weather closures and construction sites, call the twenty-four-hour CalTrans recording at (800) 427-7623.

## Road Maps

Don't venture out without road maps, unless you know exactly where you're going. The maps in this book have been provided to give you overviews of your trips, but far more detailed maps are available. Keep in mind, too, that there are alternative routes to almost all the destinations I've covered, and some might be more suitable for your trips.

Most bookstores have thorough map sections, with everything from local maps to atlases. In addition, several Web sites can provide very accurate and detailed maps of any destination or address in this book. Try mapquest.com.

## Obey the Rules of the Road

Keep in mind that speed limits and other rules of the road were written with your safety in mind. Besides, you'll enjoy your trip more if you're not in a hurry.

Generally, the speed limit on interstates in California is 70 mph, 55 mph on federal and state highways. Seat belts are required, and children who are either under five years old or who weigh less than forty pounds are required to be strapped into child-safety seats. For more information call the **California Highway Patrol** at (916) 263-3550 or the **California Motor Vehicle Department** at (916) 657-6555.

## Animals in the Roadway

One of the joys of driving through rural California is the variety of wildlife you're likely to see: deer, raccoons, coyotes, possums, rabbits, even bears, not to mention domesticated animals such as dogs, cats, sheep, and cattle. Keep your eye out for animals crossing the road, especially in the mountains in spring and fall when the deer are migrating. Remember, too, that deer very rarely travel alone. If you see a deer in or beside the road, it's almost certain that another is nearby. One might bound across the highway and out of the way, only to be followed by another, hard on its heels.

## Sleeping away from Home

Although this book is generally defined as a day-trips guide, I've provided places to bed down in most of the destinations, should you become enchanted with the area or simply too tired to drive home (never push it when you're tired; it's better to arrive home later than you planned than not all).

On the other hand, it's often difficult to find lodging at the last minute, and you're very much advised to make reservations, especially in the most common tourist areas, including the Napa and Sonoma Valleys, Lake Tahoe, San Francisco, and the gold country, particularly during the busy seasons. That includes fall, or harvest time, in the wine country, and winter, or ski season, in Lake Tahoe.

I've tried as best I could to include a range of lodging options. Bed and breakfasts can be nice, although even in the most private of them, you're still in someone else's home and are pretty much obligated to chat with other guests and keep a generally friendly demeanor. Sometimes you even have to sit with other guests at breakfast. Bed and breakfasts generally run from $100 to $150 a night for a room, more in some of the fancier ones, such as the Gaige House in Glen Ellen.

If you'd rather stay anonymous (not for illegal or immoral reasons, I'm assuming), a generic motel can be a better call. Sometimes there's nothing better than just shutting yourself off behind the door of a little mom-and-pop place or a Best Western and having your time to yourself. These usually run from $70 to $100 a night for two.

I've also included a handful of very high-end digs, for those of you looking to celebrate a special occasion or who've just been handed a

pile of cash from Regis. The Ritz-Carlton, for example, in San Francisco, has about the highest rates you'll find in this book, but for
that one-time splurge it just might be right.

All of the chambers of commerce and convention-and-visitor
bureaus listed in the back of this book under Regional Information
will be happy to send you complete listings of lodging in their areas.

# USING THIS TRAVEL GUIDE

**Highway designations:** Federal highways are designated U.S. State routes are indicated by CA.

**Hours of operation:** Hours have been omitted because they are subject to frequent change. Instead, addresses and phone numbers are provided so that you can obtain the most up-to-date information.

**Restaurants:** Restaurant prices are designated $$$ (expensive, $15 and over for an entree); $$ (moderate, $5–$15); and $ (inexpensive, $5 and under).

**Accommodations:** Room prices are designated as $$$ (expensive, over $100 for a standard room); $$ (moderate, $50–$100); and $ (inexpensive, under $50).

**Credit cards:** Most of the restaurants and accommodations in this book accept credit cards, unless noted otherwise.

---

The prices and rates listed in this guidebook were confirmed at press time. We recommend, however, that you call establishments before traveling to obtain current information.

North Day Trip 1

Paradise
Chico
191
Lake Oroville
Oroville
99
70
Delevan Natl. Wildlife Refuge
Nevada City
Grass Valley
20
Sutter Buttes
Williams
20
Marysville
Colusa Natl. Wildlife Refuge
Yuba City
70
49
Sutter Natl. Wildlife Refuge
99
Marshall Gold Discovery St. Hist. Pk.
16
70
99
Co
49
80
50
5
Sacramento
Davis
50
Silverado Trail
80
160
16
Vacaville
Sutter Creek
Courtland
Jacks
Napa
150
Ryde
Locke
12
12
Rio Vista
Isleton
80
Vallejo
Be
780
680
4
Martinez
80

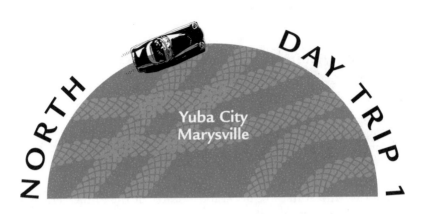

Flanked by the Coast Range to the west and the Sierra Nevada to the east, the Sacramento Valley sprawls north of Sacramento some 200 miles before meeting the mountains of northern California and southern Oregon. In the past one of the continent's most diverse natural-wildlife habitats—teeming with wildflowers, grizzly bears, wolves, and great flocks of ducks and geese that darkened the sky— the valley is now largely tamed, defined by geometric fields of rice, and farmlands and orchards laid out in rows. Principal crops include peaches, prunes, tomatoes, corn, olives, and nuts—walnuts, almonds, and pistachios—most irrigated with water from the Feather and Sacramento Rivers, the two main waterways that define the valley.

Fifty miles north of Sacramento on CA-99 and CA-70 lies the area known as the Twin Cities. Surrounded by rice paddies, fruit and nut orchards, and tomato fields, Yuba City and Marysville give visitors a sample of the tastes of the farm-rich Sacramento Valley. The traveler will discover that these two cities, with culturally diverse populations, create a unique and harmonious community unlike any in the Golden State.

The original inhabitants of Yuba and Sutter Counties were the Maidu Indians, who lived in the area for more than 10,000 years. The Maidu called the area the Inland Sea due to the flooding that occurred during the winter months from the convergence of three rivers, the Yuba, Feather, and Sacramento. Until the gold rush and creation of levees during the 1800s, this flooding helped to create some of the richest agricultural land in the valley. The name Yuba is

1

said to come from the corruption of the Spanish word *uba* referring to the grapes that grew along the banks of the rivers. Others claim *yu-ba* was the tribal name of the Maidu Indians.

## YUBA CITY

Yuba City, the Sutter County seat, is located at the former site of a Maidu village, near the confluence of the Yuba and Feather Rivers. The land, which was purchased from John Sutter in 1849, was incorporated in 1908. In 1986 Rand McNally's *Places Rated Almanac* placed Yuba City dead last, and Yuba City residents protested by burning Rand McNally maps and donning T-shirts reading, "Rand McNally, Kiss Our Buttes." Yuba City has been working hard to make improvements and was recently counted among the fastest-growing areas in Northern California.

### WHERE TO GO

**Community Memorial Museum of Sutter County.** 1333 Butte House Road, Yuba City, CA 95993.The museum is a showplace for agricultural and household artifacts, as well as baskets created by the Maidu Indians. The objects and their setting invite the viewer to investigate the everyday life of the citizens of the community. The museum offers an excellent guidebook, *Walking Tour of Historic Yuba City and Marysville,* which can be purchased for a nominal fee. The book has detailed maps and descriptions of historic buildings and sites, some of which were designed by architect Julia Morgan. The museum also has a gift shop that stocks a variety of gifts and informative books on local history and geology. The museum is closed Mondays. (530) 822-7141.

**Sunsweet.** 901 North Walton (just off CA-20), Yuba City, CA 95993. The Yuba City plant is the world's largest handler of dried prunes and dried tree fruits. The plant is capable of packaging more than 60,000 units of dried fruit per day. Products packaged by the plant include dried prunes, prune juice, cranberry juice, and bottled juice products for Snapple. Each September Sunsweet is a sponsor of the California Prune Festival, which features art, jazz, and, of course, the most creative prune-inspired cuisine in the state. Tours of the plant are available by prior appointment on Tuesday and Thursday only. To arrange a tour call (530) 751-5201.

The Grower's Store on the premises is open to the public and sells a variety of dried fruits, nuts, and gourmet food items. The store is open Monday through Saturday.

## WHERE TO SHOP

**Downtown Yuba City.** Plumas Street (just off CA-20) makes for a fun shopping experience. Stroll past newly renovated storefronts, grab a bite at **Trimble's Soda Fountain,** and sip a latte at **Java Retreat.** From April through October the Yuba City Farmer's Market offers fresh fruits and vegetables to the public on Saturday mornings. Other notable establishments include **Hello Gardener, Chili Cauldron, Decor and Design, The Underground, Candy Box, The City Cafe,** and **Runway Rags.**

**The Seedling Nursery.** 1499 Lincoln Road (just off CA-99),Yuba City, CA 95991. Voted as one of the best destinations in northern California by *Sunset* magazine, the Seedling Nursery is a definite must-see. Owner Ron Eckhard has created a variety of gardens that showcase his landscaping and plant expertise. Visitors can wander freely through the rose, water, oriental, and Shakespeare gardens. Plants and decorative items are available for sale. The nursery is open seven days a week. (530) 674-5263.

**Johnson's Farm.** 6255 Sawtell Avenue, Yuba City, CA 95991. This roadside stand is known across the county as one of the best places to purchase fruit pies and locally grown produce. More than twenty different kinds of pie are available, as well as preserves, nuts, fruits, and vegetables. The stand is open seven days a week. (530) 673-0406.

## WHERE TO EAT

**Ruthy's Bar and Grill.** Hillcrest Plaza at 229 Clark Avenue, Yuba City, CA 95991. Ruthy's features some of the finest food in the Yuba City area. Owner Steve Shelton presents a superb Sunday brunch buffet that includes roast prime rib, turkey, ham, and all the fixings. The bar and wine shop features a wide selection of California wines and microbrewed beers, as well as the best spirits available. Ruthy's is open for breakfast, lunch, and dinner Tuesday through Sunday. $$-$$$. (530) 674-2611.

**El Zarape.** 1085 Gray Avenue (off CA-20), Yuba City, CA 95991. El Zarape is one of the oldest family-owned restaurants in the area. They feature a wide selection of Mexican dishes and serve the best margaritas in town. The restaurant is open seven days a week for breakfast, lunch, and dinner. $-$$. (530) 755-2888.

**Taste of India.** 1456 Bridge Street, Yuba City, CA 95991. Yuba City is host to one of the largest Sikh parades in North America each year during the month of November. Taste of India reflects this large East Indian population through its authentic Indian cuisine and sweets. A variety of meat and vegetarian entrees are available as well as tandoori dishes. The restaurant is open Tuesday through Sunday for lunch and dinner. $$-$$$. (530) 751-5156.

## WHERE TO STAY

**The Harkey House.** 212 C Street, Yuba City, CA 95991. The house, which was built in 1874, is featured in the *Walking Tour of Historic Yuba City and Marysville*. This unique Victorian bed-and-breakfast features a balustrade veranda, hipped roof, and tall pediment windows. The sumptuous accommodations and beautiful rooms are sure to soothe the weary traveler. A choice of delicious breakfast entrees is available. $$. (530) 674-1942.

## MARYSVILLE

Marysville, the Yuba County seat, is right across the river from its sister city, Yuba City. Marysville was founded on January 18, 1850, and was named after Mary Murphy Covillaud, a survivor of the Donner Party. In 1851 during the gold rush, Marysville was the third-largest city in the state. The city has a colorful reputation and at one time had more than twenty-five working theaters. Miners came from miles around to buy provisions and spend their hard-earned diggings on whiskey and damsels of ill repute. The city also had one of the largest Chinese populations and has hosted the Bok Kai parade each spring for 118 consecutive years. The parade honors the Chinese water god Bok Kai, who is believed to control floods, irrigation, and rains. Currently, Bill Graham Presents is building a concert site on Highway 70 just outside of Marysville, and the residents hope that this new concert venue will attract tourism and help restore historic Marysville to its original gold rush splendor.

## WHERE TO GO

**Yuba-Sutter Chamber of Commerce.** 429 Tenth Street, Yuba City, CA 95901. A good place to get oriented to the Yuba City–Marysville area, this office will provide brochures on dining, lodging, and other attractions in the area. (530) 743-6501.

**Ellis Lake.** Located in the center of Marysville at B and Fourteenth Streets, Ellis Lake and its lighted fountain have been the crown jewel of the city since 1939. Originally a sprawling swamp, it was transformed by Golden Gate Park designer John McLaren and the WPA into a recreation area. Named after W. T. Ellis, a prominent Marysville citizen, the lake offers a pleasant walk, picnic areas, and pedal boats.

**Bok Kai Temple.** First and D Streets, Marysville, CA 95901. The only temple of its kind in the Western Hemisphere, the Bok Kai Temple was dedicated on March 21, 1880. According to Chinese legend Bok Kai was once a human but became a deity by devising levees to hold back floodwaters in his homeland. The temple was declared a national landmark in 1976, when it was listed in the National Register of Historic Places. Enjoy the serenity of the tree-lined First Street park and a picnic lunch by the Chinese pavilion.

**Renaissance Winery.** 8712 Marysville Road, Oregon House, CA 95962. Located in the Yuba County foothill community of Oregon House, about twenty minutes east of Marysville, the Renaissance Winery produces award-winning wines from handpicked grapes. Tours of the winery and formal rose garden can be arranged by appointment. The tasting room is open Friday and Saturday and by appointment. (800) 655-3277. Their **Bistro Restaurant,** serving fine French cuisine, is open Wednesday through Saturday for lunch. (530) 692-2938.

## WHERE TO SHOP

**Historic Downtown Marysville**. Along C and D Streets in central Marysville. Peruse a variety of original brick business buildings of early Marysville, as well as Italianate, Gothic, and Eastlake architectural styles. Many of the buildings have been renovated and house an interesting collection of small shops and storefronts. Check out the street arch at Fifth and D Streets that is a replica of one of five arches spanning D Street at the turn of the century. The originals were styled after an arch on Fillmore Street in San Francisco. As you walk along, be sure to stop at the **Candy Box** for a chocolate turtle. These delightful confections are made fresh daily and are a local favorite. Other worthy proprietors: **D Street Mercantile, Sutter Surplus, Sullivan's Saddlery, Country Emporium, Fine Arts Gallery, Times Passing Antiques,** and **Scott's Ideal Bakery.**

## WHERE TO EAT

**Diakoku.** 310 C Street, Marysville, CA 95901. Featuring Teppan style Japanese cuisine for an entertaining dining experience and an excellent selection of tempura, soba noodles, sushi, and sashimi. The restaurant also offers a full service bar. Open Tuesday through Sunday for lunch and dinner. $-$$. (530) 742-6503.

**Dragon Inn.** 1016 G Street, Marysville, CA 95901. Authentic Chinese and Sezchuan cuisine are the specialties at Dragon Inn. They feature excellent service and exotic Polynesian-style drinks such as Singapore Slings and Mai Tais. Open seven days a week, Monday through Friday for lunch and dinner, Saturday and Sunday for dinner only. $-$$. (530) 742-6923.

**Silver Dollar Saloon.** 330 First Street, Marysville, CA 95901. This historic Marysville landmark serves no-nonsense steaks, chops and burgers. On weekends local bands play live music for your dancing pleasure. Stop in, belly up to the bar, and drink in the sights, tastes, and sounds of old Marysville. Open for lunch and dinner seven days a week. $-$$. (530) 743-0007.

I-5 doglegs west out of Sacramento, passes by Sacramento International Airport, and then shoots north, making pretty much a straight run for the Oregon border. This is the heart of the valley, and though the scenery isn't particularly arresting—at least until you get way north, near Redding and Mount Shasta—the farmlands, which flank the interstate much of the way, are of vital importance to California's economy. Depending on the time of year, you'll see a huge range of crops being picked and shipped: rice, sugar beets, tomatoes, olives, almonds, cotton, corn, melons, and many others.

## SUTTER BUTTES

One landmark that will catch your eye is the Sutter Buttes. Here, forming a triangle with Colusa and Yuba City to the south and smack dab in the middle of near-sea-level flatness, is the 75-square-mile Sutter Buttes, often called the world's smallest mountain range. Seen from the road, the range looks like a long series of peaks running north to south, whereas in reality, they actually form a sort of circle, enclosing interior valleys and meadows. In winter the 2,000-foot mountaintops are often dusted with snow, making even more dramatic,the relief against the valley floor.

Created by a volcanic uplift about two and a half million years ago, held sacred by local Indian tribes, and used as landmarks for centuries by explorers and travelers, the Buttes presently are largely

7

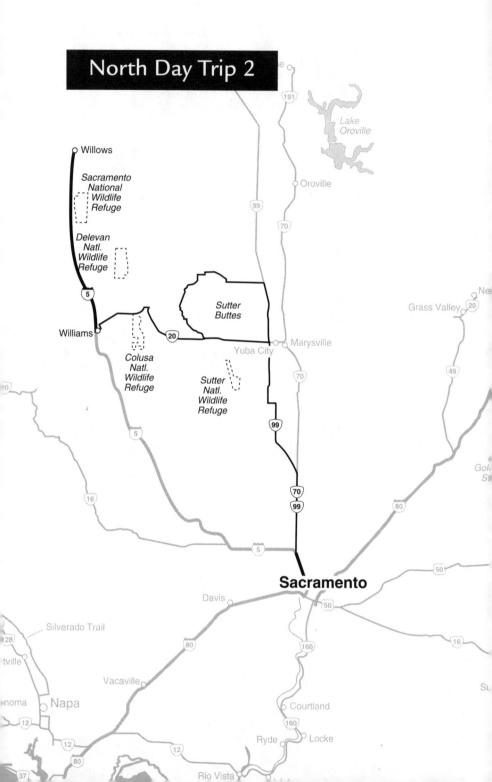

# North Day Trip 2

Willows

*Sacramento
National
Wildlife
Refuge*

*Delevan
Natl.
Wildlife
Refuge*

5

Williams

*Colusa
Natl.
Wildlife
Refuge*

*Sutter
Buttes*

20

*Sutter
Natl.
Wildlife
Refuge*

*Lake
Oroville*

191

Oroville

99

70

Grass Valley

20

Yuba City

Marysville

70

49

99

70
99

5

16

80

**Sacramento**

Davis

50

80

160

16

*Silverado Trail*

28

tville

Vacaville

Napa

noma

12

12

12

80

37

Courtland

160

Ryde

Locke

Rio Vista

Gol
S

Ne

20

80

50

5

Su

privately owned but do offer limited opportunities for hiking and exploring, as well as excellent vistas of the surrounding Sacramento Valley.

You can get a perspective on the Buttes by circumnavigating them by car or bicycle, about a 40-mile trip. From I-5 go east on CA-20 to Acacia Road and drive north to Butte House Road, where you'll head west.

Because Sutter Buttes are mostly on private property, public access is limited to guided tours. The Middle Mountain Foundation, a nonprofit organization dedicated to preserving the range, offers an array of hikes, from gentle walks through the rolling meadows to rugged ascents of the upper peaks. You must call ahead to book a tour. Cost is about $25 per person for a six-hour hike. For reservations and more information, call (530) 846-5142.

# SACRAMENTO NATIONAL WILDLIFE REFUGE COMPLEX

Because much of the Sacramento Valley lies beneath the great Western Flyway, this is one of the best places in the country to view migrating birds, which stop in the marshy wetlands and rest along their journey. From mid-November through January, fields in the valley are often virtually carpeted with Canada geese, snow geese, swans, and many species of duck, in addition to egrets and great blue herons. Meanwhile, red-tailed hawks and other birds of prey watch from treetops or swoop down from the skies to pluck mice from the fields.

The Sacramento National Wildlife Refuge Complex comprises five separate refuges and is an attempt to preserve what little is left of the original wetlands that the waterfowl have relied on for thousands of years. Though established largely for migrating birds, the refuges are also home to many other species of wildlife, including coyotes, rabbits, and deer, as well as turtles, snakes, and lizards, and they provide visitors with excellent opportunities to view how these animals make their homes—even if only temporarily—in the reedy marshlands of the Sacramento Valley. The best months for seeing the waterfowl are November, December, and January, although the refuges are open year-round, and it's rare that a visit won't result in a rewarding and satisfying outing, whether from your car, the observation platforms, or the walking trails throughout. Be sure to bring your camera and binoculars.

A good place to begin your tour of the refuges is at the **Sacramento National Wildlife Refuge** visitor center just south of Willows, about 90 miles north of Sacramento, just off I-5 at 752 County Road 99W. You can also get there by taking Norman Road west from Princeton. The visitor center has wildlife exhibits, a bookstore, and interpretive kiosks, and you can also pick up maps and information about the other five refuges. Open daily October through March and weekends the rest of the year. Small entrance fee.

The other refuges in the complex include the **Delevan National Wildlife Refuge** (take Maxwell Road east from I-5 or west from CA-45); **Colusa National Wildlife Refuge** (take Lonestar Road south from CA-20 west of Colusa); and **Sutter National Wildlife Refuge** (take CA-20 east from Colusa to Tarke Road south, then McGrath to Oswald). No entrance fees at these refuges.

For more information write Sacramento National Wildlife Refuge Complex, 752 County Road 99W, Willows, CA 95988, or call (530) 934-2801.

## WHERE TO EAT

**Granzella's Delicatessen.** Corner of Main and Sixth, Williams, CA 95987. This little delicatessen and restaurant—out in the middle of proverbial nowhere—is a must not only for hungry passers-through but for all who want to stock their pantries or fill their picnic baskets for a wonderful meal farther on down the road. In addition to excellent sandwiches made to order, on some of the best and freshest bread this side of Fisherman's Wharf, the deli serves homemade soups and a wide range of pasta salads. Bonus: While you wait for your sandwich to be made, wander toward the back of the store and check out the dozen or so different kinds of olives, in huge jars open for sampling. If you're lucky, they'll even have an open jar of marinated garlic cloves. There's also a refrigerator case stocked with unique beers and ales from around the world. If you'd rather sit down to eat, the adjacent restaurant serves pizza, pastas, sandwiches, and soups. At the bar in back, you can get a burger and fries and watch a football game on television while shooting a game of pool. $-$$. (530) 473-5496.

## WHERE TO STAY

**Granzella's Inn.** 391 North Sixth Street, Williams, CA 95987. The success of Granzella's deli spawned the recent construction of this large (two-story, forty-five-room) motel next door. Rooms are good sized; some suites available. $$. (530) 473-3310.

**Stage Stop Motel.** 330 North Seventh Street, Williams, CA 95987. This unpretentious little motel has been a Williams mainstay for years, providing good, clean rest for weary I-5-corridor travelers. Twenty-five rooms. $-$$. (530) 473-2281.

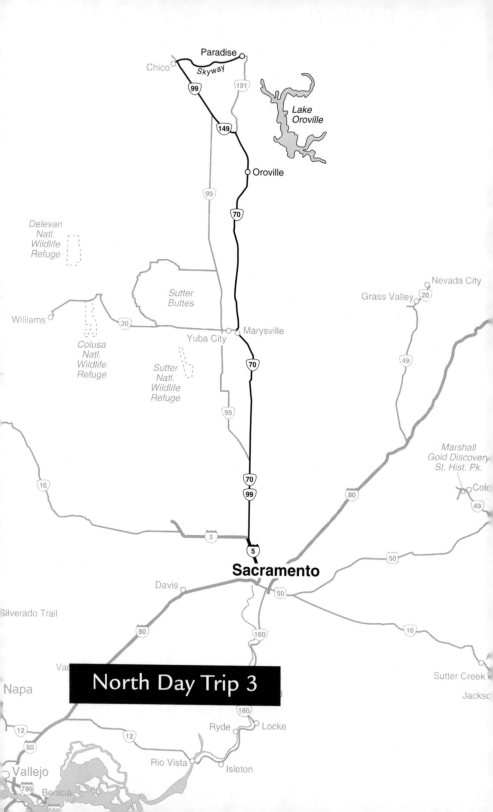

North Day Trip 3

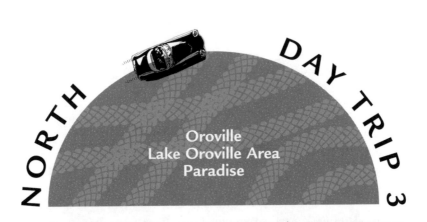

## OROVILLE

About 90 miles north of Sacramento via Highways 99 and 70, Oroville is the seat of Butte County and the focal point of some of northern California's most fascinating history. During the early 1860s the area was home to more than 10,000 Chinese, most of whom came to work the nearby mines and who dutifully sent home all but what they needed to survive of their paltry paychecks. Later, the Chinese worked the railroads, and then the farms and ranches of anglo settlers; often they were victims of racism, manifesting itself in abuse and even murder.

Oroville is also where Ishi, the famous Yahi Indian—literally the last of his tribe—left one world and entered another. Late one evening in 1911, he appeared near a corral beside a slaughterhouse. He was said to be partly clothed and looking malnourished. Locals tried in vain to communicate with him, but no one had ever heard the language he spoke, even those who knew some Native American tongues. Turns out, Ishi's family and tribe had all died off, and as white settlement encroached onto traditional Yahi land, Ishi finally felt he could no longer live in his world.

Originally locked up by the Oroville sheriff, Ishi was soon sent to Berkeley. There, he became the subject of an intense study by anthropologist Alfred Kroeber, who dedicated much of his life to learning about northern California Native Americans largely through what he learned from Ishi, who led Kroeber and others into the backcountry and demonstrated the hunting and fishing techniques of his tribe.

Since 1967, Oroville has been best known as the site of Lake Oroville, formed by Oroville Dam, which is part of the California Water Project, providing flood control, irrigation water, and electricity for the state. At present Oroville is home to about 12,000 people, including a very large number of Hmong and Mien, who came to the area from the Cambodian and Laotian mountains following the Viet Nam War.

## WHERE TO GO

. **Oroville Area Chamber of Commerce.** 1789 Montgomery Street, Oroville, CA 95965. Stop in for maps to the area and details on Lake Oroville, as well as complete listings of lodging and eating options in town. You can also get relocation information. (530) 538–2542.

**Chinese Temple.** 1500 Broderick, Oroville, CA 95965. Built in 1863 by and for Chinese laborers who had come to California to work in the mines, this ornate and fascinating temple is on the National Register of Historic Places and is a must-see for anyone interested in the diversity of contributions to California history. Honoring the three main faiths of the workers, Buddhism, Taoism, and Confucianism, the temple is full of artifacts—tapestries, puppets, and earthenware—from its early days and is still a holy place of worship for the remaining Chinese in the area. Open Monday through Thursday with limited hours. Small admission fee. (530) 538–2496.

**Butte County Pioneer Museum.** 2322 Montgomery Street, Oroville, CA 95965. This small museum near downtown Oroville commemorates the area's Native American, mining, and early twentieth-century history. Displays include mining equipment, Victorian clothing, doll collections, and historical photos. Open Sunday afternoons only, February through June and September through November. Also open by appointment for group tours. (530) 538–2542.

## WHERE TO EAT

Not a whole lot to choose from here—a lot of folks drive to Chico to go to dinner—but there is a handful of the ubiquitous franchise fast-food places located at the freeway exits.

**The Depot.** 2191 High Street, Oroville, CA 95965. This classic steak-and-seafood joint has been a local favorite for years. Salad bar and children's menu available. Open Monday through Saturday for lunch and dinner, Sunday for dinner only. $$–$$$. (530) 534–9101.

## WHERE TO STAY

**Lake Oroville Bed and Breakfast.** 240 Sunday Drive, Berry Creek, CA 95916. Built in 1992 by Ron and Cheryl Damberger, who fled the chaos of the Bay Area, this out-of-the-way bed-and-breakfast offers the peace and serenity the couple found. All six rooms have private baths, and all but one have spas. Views of the lake and surrounding foothills, studded with spreading oak and evergreens. Full breakfast is included. (530) 589–0700.

# LAKE OROVILLE AREA

Lake Oroville was created in 1967 with the completion of Oroville Dam, today one of the county's most striking "landmarks." The lake, fed by the many branches and forks of the Feather River, is characterized by scores of narrow fingers and inlets, some winding deep into shadowy canyons. The total shoreline is 176 miles, and the lake covers 16,400 acres. A favorite of houseboaters, bass fishers, and water-skiers, the lake, and the goings-on there, has a great impact on the surrounding area. Not only does it affect recreation and tourism, but local farmers and ranchers depend on water from Lake Oroville for irrigation.

**Lake Oroville State Recreation Area.** Encompassing more than 30,000 acres, this state park is a favorite of campers, fishers, water-skiers, and sightseers from throughout the north state. Drive-in and boat-in-only camping are available, and you can rent houseboats by the day or week. Depending on the time of season, you can fish for small- and large-mouth bass, trout, and salmon, and legend even has it that some lunker sturgeon lurk in the lake's depths, planted just after the dam was completed.

**Lake Oroville Visitors Center.** Learn about the lake's history, as well as the history of the surrounding area at this very nice visitor center perched on the bank high above the water. In addition, learn about the area's natural history and the history of the Native Americans who in the past depended on the river for much of their sustenance. Among the videos available is one on Ishi, the last Yahi Indian to survive white settlement (see above). The visitor center is open daily 9:00 A.M. to 5:00 P.M. Admission is free. To get there take Highway 162 east from Oroville to Kelly Ridge Road, and watch for the signs. (530) 538-2219.

**Feather River Fish Hatchery.** The completion of Oroville Dam and the subsequent filling-in of Lake Oroville in 1967 destroyed miles and miles of spawning beds of chinook salmon and steelhead, the runs of which were some of the largest on the west coast. The Feather River Fish Hatchery was built in hopes of keeping these runs from becoming extinct.

The hatchery is open during the fall spawning season (September through November), when you can view monstrous salmon leaping high into the air as they navigate the fish ladder and also as they prepare to procreate, apparently unselfconsciously, behind observation glass. Open daily. Admission is free. To get there take Highway 70 north from Oroville to the Nelson Road exit and watch for the signs. For information call (530) 538-2222. To arrange guided tours call (530) 534-2306.

**Feather Falls Scenic Area.** The sixth-highest waterfall in the United States—and outside Yosemite, the highest in the state—this impressive falls pours 640 feet over a granite cliff to crash in spumy spray on the rocks below. Located about 20 miles northeast of Oroville, Feather Falls offers an excellent excursion into some gorgeous backcountry, especially in late spring and early summer, when the wildflowers are in bloom and the snowmelt flows most dramatically and powerfully over the cliff. A large fenced-in viewing area is ideal for picture taking. (*Note:* The hike to Feather Falls is not for young children or anyone unable to negotiate five-plus hours of narrow trails and steep switchbacks.) To get to Feather Falls take Forbestown Road east from Oroville to Lumpkin Road and watch for the signs. For more information call the Oroville Area Chamber of Commerce at (530) 583-2542.

**Cherokee.** Butte County's best "ghost town," Cherokee was named for the Cherokee Indians who came west from Georgia in the 1850s to mine for gold in the Oroville area. By the early 1870s as much as $5 million in gold was being taken from the area annually, largely hydraulically, and the landscape still bears the scars where entire mountainsides were washed away with the high-pressure water guns.

About all that's left of the once-thriving town are the crumbling walls of the stores and the jail, and it's fun to wander the overgrown streets and imagine them bustling with miners a century and a half ago. To get there take Highway 70 north from Oroville about 10 miles and watch for the sign to Cherokee Road on the right. The road continues across the top of Table Mountain—gorgeous with wildflowers in spring, perfect for picnicking—and winds back into Oroville the back way.

## PARADISE

Perched atop a Sierra Nevada foothill ridge just north of Oroville, Paradise is a small community made up of a disproportionately large number of retirees, many of whom have fled the traffic and congestion of the Bay Area and southern California for a slower-paced life in the pines. In addition, Paradise is home to many Chico workers, who make the 20-minute easy commute from their homes on "the ridge" to the valley, preferring the cooler foothill climate: When Chico's baking in 100-degree summer heat, it's generally at least ten degrees cooler on "the ridge," and on a cold winter day, it might be raining in Chico and snowing in Paradise, whose elevation rises from about 1,700 to 2,200 feet.

Paradise locals pride themselves on several things: a fierce independence, which often manifests itself in political conservatism; the town's gold-mining history, celebrated each July with Gold Nugget Days; and a simple, unadorned lifestyle perfectly befitting the large number of retirees.

To get to Paradise from Oroville, take Highway 70 north about 7 miles to CA-191 and watch for the turn-off on the left. You can also go north on Highway 99 to Chico and take Skyway, the main road up the ridge. You can also turn off Sky just a mile up and go up through Butte Creek Canyon on Honey Run Road and past the Honey Run Covered Bridge. It will take you quite a bit longer—

maybe forty minutes as opposed to twenty—but the narrow, winding road offers gorgeous views of Butte Creek tumbling through the canyon, while the switchbacky ascent up the ridgeside, often completely canopied with trees, provides a dramatic entry through Paradise's back door. *A suggestion:* Since the views from the Skyway can themselves be quite breathtaking—of sheer cliffs and deep canyons—go up the Skyway and come back down through the canyon, or vice versa.

## WHERE TO GO

**Paradise Chamber of Commerce and Visitors Center.** 5550 Skyway, Paradise, CA 95969. Stop in here for information on everything from local antiques stores to relocation. In addition, pick up maps highlighting nearby campgrounds, lakes, and golf courses. (530) 877–9356.

   **Gold Nugget Museum.** 502 Pearson Road, Paradise, CA 95969. Named for the famous fifty-four-pound nugget discovered in nearby Magalia, this museum celebrates the history of Paradise and much of the foothill ridge on which the town is built. In addition to pioneer exhibits from mining tools to doll collections, displays include a blacksmith shop, a working replication of a sluice box, and Native American basketry and clothing. Each April the museum is the focus of the town's Gold Nugget Days, when docents dress in period costume, kids can pan for gold, and picnickers are treated to live music beside the creek that runs through the museum's grounds. Open Wednesday through Sunday. (530) 872–8722.

   **Honey Run Covered Bridge.** Coming into Paradise the back way, stop in at this restored 1887 covered bridge, open to foot traffic only, over Butte Creek. You'll find picnic facilities and, for the stout of heart, some nice swimming holes. There's also excellent trout, salmon, and steelhead fishing, though make sure you check local restrictions. Small fee for day use.

## WHERE TO SHOP

The only real reason to go shopping in Paradise would be to go "antiquing." Presumably related to the disproportionately large number of senior citizens in Paradise, the town's many antiques stores can provide a pleasant afternoon of browsing. You'll find everything from quality armoires and dining sets to the proverbial dinner- and flatware (maybe even a baby spoon commemorating Idaho!), to Grandpa's old bass plugs, to knitted samplers testifying to the goodness of home and family values. Most of the shops have lists available of the other antiques stores in the area, as well as maps showing how to find them.

**Jeannie's.** 8672 Skyway, Paradise, CA 95969. Probably the best place to start. With luck you just might happen on a full set of silver from an estate sale or a quality lamp on consignment. (530) 877-6650.

## WHERE TO EAT

**Ivar's.** 13915 South Park Drive, Magalia, CA 95954. Folks come from all over Butte County to this homey little restaurant overlooking the Pines golf course just a few miles above Paradise. In addition to the excellent dinners, with entrees ranging from Jack Daniels-marinated pork chops to fettuccini primavera, Ivar's also offers a very good Sunday brunch, including crepes, omelets, and French toast. Dinner hours are Wednesday through Sunday from 5:00 to 10:00 P.M., and brunch is served Sunday 10:00 A.M. to 2:00 P.M. $$. (530) 873-4878.

**La Comida.** 6153 Skyway, Paradise, CA 95969. For consistently good and inexpensive Mexican food—though perhaps more "Americanized" than some—try this little cafeteria-style restaurant, in business for more than twenty years. $-$$. (530) 877-5246.

## WHERE TO STAY

**Ponderosa Gardens Motel.** 7010 Skyway, Paradise, CA 95969. This is a mid-sized (forty-eight units) motel conveniently located on Paradise's main drag. Amenities include a pool and spa, and rates include a continental breakfast. $$. (888) 727-3423.

**Paradise Inn.** 5423 Skyway, Paradise, CA 95969. This is a much smaller facility (seventeen rooms), although some of the units have kitchenettes. Also conveniently located on the Skyway. $. (530) 877-2127.

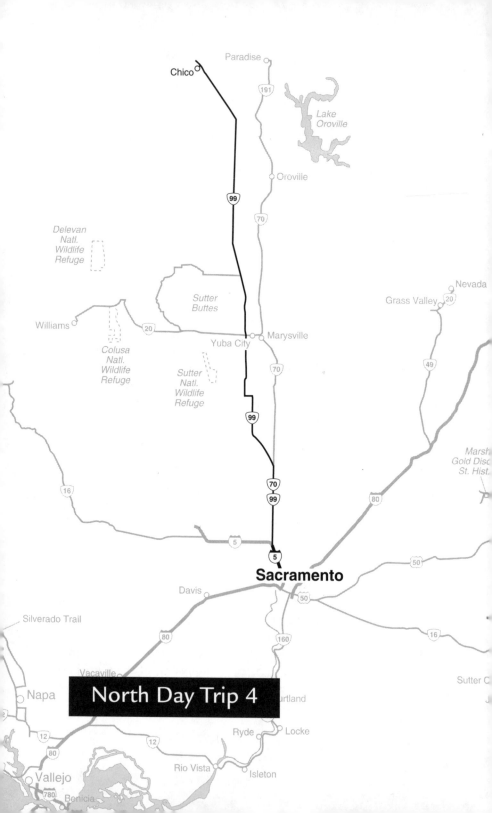

Paradise

Chico

191

Lake
Oroville

99

Oroville

70

Delevan
Natl.
Wildlife
Refuge

Nevada

Grass Valley    20

Sutter
Buttes

20

Williams

Colusa
Natl.
Wildlife
Refuge

Yuba City    Marysville

49

70

Sutter
Natl.
Wildlife
Refuge

99

Marsh
Gold Disc
St. Hist.

16

70
99

80

5

5

50

Sacramento

Davis

50

Silverado Trail

16

80

160

Vacaville

**North Day Trip 4**

rtland

Sutter C

Napa

12

Ryde    Locke

80

12

Vallejo    Rio Vista    Isleton

780    Benicia

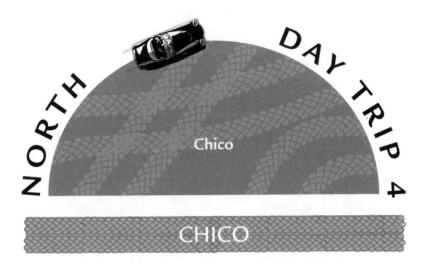

# CHICO

About 90 miles north of Sacramento, Chico is a classic valley town with an important distinction: It's the site of the California State University, Chico, home to 15,000 undergraduate and graduate students taking advantage of the school's excellent computer-science, nursing, engineering, agricultural, and other programs. Originally a normal (or teacher-training) school, CSU, Chico was founded in 1887 and remains the north state's primary institution for training teachers who plan to go into the public-school arena. It's also Chico's largest employer.

Because the university is right downtown, and because a huge proportion of the student body lives within a mile of campus, the little town is defined largely by students. You'd be hard pressed to find another town in California with more bars and live-music venues per capita, and on Thursday, Friday, and Saturday nights—especially in springtime and early fall—the streets come alive with young people out for a good time.

That's not to say the community is entirely student oriented. Indeed, though students and locals get along quite well for the most part, most locals love the periods between semesters, when a good proportion of the students pack up and head back to the Bay Area or to southern California. Yet no one can be too damning of the students: Many longtime locals—attorneys, teachers, small-business owners, and realtors—originally came to Chico to attend the university.

## WHERE TO GO

**Chico Chamber of Commerce.** 300 Salem, Chico, CA 95928. Plan to stop by this little office just 2 blocks off Main Street to pick up brochures and maps that will lead you to the town's and area's many attractions. Especially useful are the maps detailing the self-guided walking and bicycling tours, which will take you from historic homes to wooded parklands. Open weekdays. (530) 891–5556.

**Bidwell Mansion State Historic Park.** 525 Esplanade, Chico, CA 95926. This is the home of General John and Annie Bidwell, the town's founders. John came to the area in 1860 with money he'd made in the California gold rush and bought 26,000 acres of land on which he developed orchards and farmland. In 1865 he built the mansion, a twenty-six-room Victorian in the style of an Italian villa. The 130-acre California State University was founded in 1887 as a teachers' college on land Bidwell donated, and many landmarks still bear the Bidwell moniker. In addition to the mansion, there's a museum and small book/gift store. Open daily. (530) 895–6144.

**Chico Museum.** 141 Salem, Chico, CA 95928. This is an excellent place to get a sense of local color and history. Learn about the important contributions Chinese immigrants made to late nineteenth- and early-twentieth-century Butte County, as well as how they maintained much of their own culture in an oftentimes hostile environment. In addition, rotating exhibits offer insights into the town's early settlement and development. Open Wednesday through Sunday. (530) 891–4336.

**Stansbury Home.** 307 West Fifth Street, Chico, CA 95928. Built in 1883, this striking Italianate Victorian was home to one of Chico's first physicians, Dr. Oscar Stansbury, and is listed on the National Register of Historic Places. It's open for free, guided thirty-minute tours on weekends and special occasions. Highlights include the Victorian Christmas and the ice-cream socials on summer evenings, which give visitors a chance to imagine life in another, far less complicated time. The house contains many of the original furnishings, as well as Dr. Stansbury's primitive medical tools and equipment. (530) 895–3848.

**Bidwell Park.** If the creek and sprawling woods of Bidwell Park look familiar, don't be alarmed: This is where Warner Brothers' 1937 *The Adventures of Robin Hood* was filmed and Robin and his merry

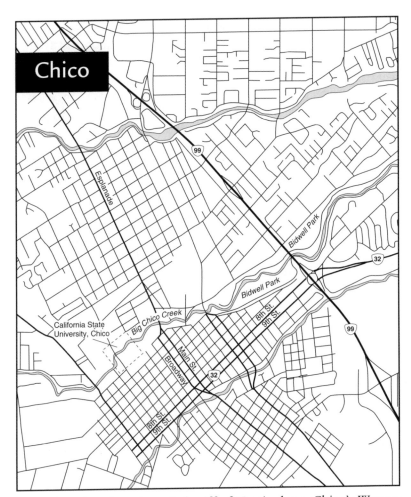

men plotted against the evil sheriff of Nottingham. Chico's Warner Street was named for the film company, and old-timers still recall sitting creekside and watching Errol Flynn's famous log-bridge swordfight and Olivia deHaviland racing horseback through the sycamores. (530) 895-4972.

Currently, the 3,670-acre park—the third-largest municipal park in the country—is home to swimming holes, jogging paths, children's playgrounds, softball fields, a nature center, picnic areas, and, of course, equestrian trails. "Lower Park," the most accessible part of the park, includes a narrow swath of land—New York's Central Park-like—pointing east from downtown Chico. The two developed swimming holes, One Mile and Five Mile, were so named for their distance from Bidwell Mansion. "Upper Park," on the other hand, is rugged and undeveloped, the road into which is only partly paved. And though you don't necessarily need a Humvee to drive in, the road is extremely rough and very hard on automobiles. The best way in is by foot, mountain bike, or horse. *A word of caution:* The swimming holes in Upper Park might look inviting, but they're extremely dangerous and have claimed many lives over the years. Swift currents dive under volcanic boulders, trapping even the strongest of swimmers. (530) 895–4972.

## WHERE TO EAT

Chico has a wide range of eateries, from pizza places catering to cash-poor students to upscale, linen-napkin restaurants where dinner for two, with a bottle of wine, will run $75 to $100. The 6-block downtown area alone contains some twenty different spots where you can get good food at reasonable prices.

In addition, there are several excellent Mexican restaurants on the highway between Sacramento and Chico, and these inexpensive little eateries are perfect for filling up after a day exploring the north valley.

**Sierra Nevada Taproom and Restaurant.** 1075 East Twentieth Street, Chico, CA 95926. If you're going to have one lunch or dinner out in Chico, this is the place. One of the country's original microbreweries, Sierra Nevada long ago grew out of that category and is now the tenth-largest brewery in the United States. Though it has expanded from its original warehouse location into a mind-boggling, huge complex, it has maintained its integrity, and taste, and consistently wins national awards for its beers and ales.

Tours of the brewery are available, and the restaurant is open six days a week for lunch and dinner and Sunday for brunch. Many of the dishes include beer in the ingredients—the fish and chips are cooked in a Pale Ale batter—and you can also get pastas, steaks, and fresh seafood. Beer connoisseurs should try the "sampler," a small taste of each of seven or eight of the available beers (many are seasonal only). $$. (530) 345-2739.

**The Black Crow Grill and Taproom.** 209 Salem, Chico, CA 95928. A favorite among local businesspeople as well as Chico state employees, the Crow serves excellent food in a lively atmosphere directly across the street from the university. Specials often include fresh fish and innovative pasta dishes, whereas standbys—salads, burgers, and beef dishes—will never disappoint. Open daily for lunch and dinner. $$-$$$. (530) 892-1391.

**Tres Hombres Long Bar and Grill.** 100 Broadway, Chico, CA 95928. In a town with well over a dozen Mexican restaurants, we could debate endlessly which is the best—most are *very* good. "Tres," however, located right downtown about 50 yards from California State University, Chico, offers without a doubt the best location, with gigantic picture windows on two sides (it's a corner building) to take full advantage. Friday and Saturday nights, this lively cantina-style restaurant is packed with students and locals, who celebrate the week's end—in the bar with chips and margaritas, in a private booth with a full-course dinner, or bellied up to the horseshoe-shaped grill for fish tacos or quesadillas. Open six days a week for lunch and dinner and Sunday for brunch. $$. (530) 342-0425.

**Christian Michaels Ristorante.** 192 East Third Street, Chico, CA 95928. One of the nicest restaurants in Chico, and offering an extensive menu and wine list, this relatively new restaurant is tough to beat. Entrees range from cioppino and lamb to seared ahi and filet mignon on garlic mashed potatoes. Open weekdays for lunch and daily for dinner. $$-$$$. (530) 894-4005.

## WHERE TO EAT
## ON THE WAY BACK TO SACRAMENTO

**El Tamborazo.** 1574 Highway 99, Gridley, CA 95948 (in the Safeway shopping center on the east side of the road). Located in the little farming community of Gridley, about a half hour south of Chico, this is one of the best Mexican restaurants around. A highlight here is spicy marinated vegetables for munchies, instead of the usual chips and salsa, jars of carrots, peppers, and cauliflower pieces are offered to each table of diners. In addition to the very good burritos and tacos, you can also get carne asada, chile verde, and fajitas. Open for lunch and dinner daily. $-$$. (530) 846-2041.

**Betty's.** 10180 Highway 99, Live Oak, CA 95953. If you didn't know better, you'd buzz right by this little place perhaps without even noticing it. That would be a mistake, however, as locals know this is one of the best Mexican restaurants in an area known for good Mexican food. Many in-the-know passersby stop in just for the famous to-go orders of chips and salsa. Also recommended: the chile colorado, chimichanga, and, if you're up to it, the menudo. Open daily for lunch and dinner, serving breakfast weekends only. $-$$. (530) 695-3535.

## WHERE TO STAY

**Esplanade Bed-and-Breakfast.** 620 Esplanade, Chico, CA 95926. Directly across the street from Bidwell Mansion and less than a quarter mile from both downtown Chico and California State University, Chico, this little bed-and-breakfast offers the most convenient lodging in town. (530) 345-8084.

**Best Western Heritage Inn.** 25 Heritage Lane, Chico, CA 95926. Located right off Highway 99 (Cohasset exit), this large facility offers clean rooms and convenience—it's about a five-minute drive to downtown or to the campus. $$. (530) 894-8600.

Grass Valley
Nevada City

Nestled in the foothills above the central valley, at the heart of California's northern gold country, Grass Valley and Nevada City are towns that still recall the forty-niner era. An hour to the east of Sacramento on I-80 and up "the hill" (as locals refer to the Sierra Nevada mountain range), these small communities are like a step back to the Victorian west. A mere 3 miles apart from each other, both Grass Valley and Nevada City have worked to form a historical community that takes you back to gold rush days.

At Christmas both towns go all out for winter festivities and close down their main thoroughfares to celebrate the season. You can expect carolers, crafters, mulled cider, roasting chestnuts, and tons of people (some in Victorian attire). Nevada City dubs its event Victorian Christmas and holds it every Wednesday in the month of December. Grass Valley holds up the mistletoe over Mill Street for Cornish Christmas for four Fridays before Christmas. Both cities are alight with gas lamps and trim adornments for the festivities. Contact the chamber of commerce in each town for additional information.

To get to the Grass Valley/Nevada City area, take I-80 about 30 miles east from Sacramento to Auburn and go north on CA-49. Grass Valley is another 25 miles north at the junction of CA-49 and CA-20.

# Northeast Day Trip 1

# GRASS VALLEY

## WHERE TO GO

**Lola Montez House.** 248 Mill Street, Grass Valley, CA 94945. One-time countess and general rabble-rouser, Lola Montez was a sort of gold rush celebrity. From 1852 to 1855 she resided in the building that now houses the chamber of commerce. A quaint structure at the far end of Mill Street, the **Grass Valley Chamber of Commerce** is easy to miss, but I wouldn't suggest it. If nothing else, drop by to have an employee tell you all about the infamous Miss Montez, who was once mistress to a Bavarian king and came to gold-fever Grass Valley with monkeys and a pet bear in tow. Nab one of those handy-dandy walking-tour leaflets for Grass Valley, and it will take you on a building-by-building trek through town with a short history on the origin of each. Open Monday through Saturday. (800) 655–4667.

**Mill Street.** Just a few miles away from Broad Street, Grass Valley's center strip is also a tribute to yesteryear. Tipping its hat to the heritage of the mother lode, this shopping section has been revamped in the Old West style. There is also some beautiful Art Deco influence in the structure of the Del Oro movie house at the end of the street. Perpendicular to this drag is Main Street, which also houses shops and some fine eateries and provides nice browsing opportunities. Antiquing is especially easy in this sector of town, with half a dozen or so quality shops peppering Mill and the adjacent streets.

**Empire Mine State Historic Park.** 10791 East Empire Street (Empire Street exit off CA–49), Grass Valley, CA 95945. At the heart of what made this area prosper is the mining industry. Grass Valley has the distinct honor of laying claim to the oldest and richest gold mine in California. The hardrock miners that came to this area from Cornwall in the late 1870s are highlighted in the park's museum and movie presentations. You can get a little more in touch with those Cornish miners by peering deep into restored and partially lit mine shaft. To get a sense of the kind of luxury the gold industry afforded its barons, you can step inside the elegant "cottage" of Empire Mine owner William Bourn, Jr. The surrounding grounds are expansive and impressive with rose gardens, fountains, and seemingly endless, winding pathways. For the less sedate grapple around in the historic mining yard as long as you avoid those rusty mining machine edges. When it is warm, take off with a self-guiding brochure (provided in the museum) and explore the hiking trails skimming the outside of the park. Open daily. Small admission fee. (530) 273-8522.

## WHERE TO EAT

**Villa Venezia.** 124 Bank Street, Grass Valley, CA 95945. Italian food with flair. For the sophisticated diner this upscale restaurant is located in The Stewart House, a restored two-story Victorian that dates from the 1880s. The warm atmosphere is scrumptious, and the food takes off from there. House specialty is the Linguini di Mare: red-sauce pasta smothered in mussels, clams, and calamari. Serving lunch and dinner. Closed Mondays. $$$. (530) 273-3555.

    **Frank's Pizza Pan.** 122 East Main Street, Grass Valley, CA 95945. Where the locals go to grub. A little hole in the wall where you can eat your greasy, filling, fresh, and tasty pie and feel right at home. $. (530) 273-4622.

## WHERE TO STAY

**Holiday Lodge AAA Motel.** 1221 East Main Street, Grass Valley, CA 95945. Cheapest rooms in town. Located on the way to the Brunswick commercial basin, the motel is clean and impersonal, as you would expect. The staff is extremely friendly, and you get the standard continental breakfast in the lobby each morning. If you are just looking for a place to lay your head and are feeling frugal, this is your best bet. Pool in the summer and sauna year-round. $-$$. (530) 273-4406.

# NEVADA CITY

## WHERE TO GO

**Ott's Assay Office.** 132 Main Street, Nevada City, CA 95959. This area has an obsession with the past and even plunks its public offices in historical landmarks. Residing in the beautiful red-brick Assay

Office just off Broad Street, the **Nevada City Chamber of Commerce** comes equipped with everything an inquisitive tourist might desire, from pamphlets to postcards. Most useful is the free walking-tour leaflet filled with stops that aren't shops but still worth mulling over. It will guide you through the Chinese Quarter along upper Commercial Street, which dates from the 1850s. It will also direct you to the town's two glorious firehouses erected in 1861. Call toll-free or visit the chamber of commerce located conveniently in the heart of town. Open Monday through Saturday. There is also a gallery featuring local artists on the second story of this building that is worth a look. (800) 655-6569.

**Broad Street.** Lined on both sides with gold rush architecture and complete with Victorian-style gas lamps, this main drag runs you straight up the biggest hill in town. Don't be fooled by this avenue's name, however; it is another throwback to the 1840s, when a roadway that will now barely accommodate two cars was considered massive. On a busy day it is best to leave your auto in the public lot at the base of the hill and make the short trek across the bridge rather than wrestling with the tight-fit parallel parking of the street slope. Shops along this street are brimming with the work of local artisans and artists as well as clothes, candy, toys, and every kind of home decoration imaginable. If you have exhausted yourself browsing through the shops of a bevy of merchants, you can swing into the coffeehouse/used bookstore at the top of the hill. Have a cup of joe, read a passage or two, and take in the beautiful spread of the town below.

**Nevada Theatre.** 401 Broad Street, Nevada City, CA 95959. The oldest building in California to be erected as a theater, this 1865 brick beauty still holds performances. The theater is home to The Foothill Theatre Company, which the *Sacramento News and Review* hailed as "the best reason to leave Sacramento in the dust." The company puts on various types of plays throughout the year. Ticket information can be obtained at (888) 730-8587. The Nevada Theatre is also the spot for the Nevada Theatre Film Series, with movies mostly of the independent and art-house variety. For show times call (530) 274-3456.

**Indian Springs Vineyard Tasting Room.** 303 Broad Street, Nevada City, CA 95959. A little bit of Napa Valley in Nevada City. Nevada County's largest vineyard, Indian Springs wants to get the word out about its award-winning wines. The Broad Street tasting room is beautiful, featuring fine stained-wood workmanship and a centralized long bar for comfortable tasting. The variety of blends provide something for everyone to sip, while the reasonable rates might allow you to walk away with a bit of the winery's handiwork. Closed Tuesday. (530) 478-1068.

## WHERE TO EAT

**Friar Tuck's Restaurant and Bar.** 111 North Pine Street (just off Broad Street), Nevada City, CA 95945. An elegant eatery that is famous for its fondues. Order the hot-oil fondue and dip away with steak, meatballs, shrimps, and scallops—or plunge vegetable medleys and bread tears into the alpine cheese or Neufchâtel fondue. The roast duck is also popular. $$$. (530) 265-9093.

**National Hotel.** 211 Broad Street, Nevada City, CA 95959. Dominating the main boulevard is California's oldest continuously operating hotel. The National's Victorian Dining Room is a beautiful place to grab a bite. The exquisite back bar is more than a hundred years old and was crafted for a private mansion before it was installed in the hotel. Breakfast, lunch, and dinner served; champagne brunch on Sundays. There are also horse-and-carriage rides available directly in front of the dining room if you get the urge to trot around town after being immersed in the historic grandeur during your meal. $$-$$$. (530) 265-4551.

## WHERE TO STAY

**Northern Queen Inn.** 400 Railroad Avenue (right off CA-49 and 20, Sacramento Street exit), Nevada City, CA 95959. A reasonably priced place with lots of space, trees, and style. You can opt for a guest room that features all the usual amenities, or step up your stay a notch to a two-story chalet. The inn's Trolley Junction Restaurant has a nice waterfall view and the option of eating in the stationary private dining car. An authentic narrow-gauge railroad also takes tours from the Northern Queen to historic sights nearby, including the former home of the Maidu Indians and a Chinese cemetery. $$. (530) 265-5824.

**Grandmere's Inn.** 449 Broad Street, Nevada City, CA 95959. A bed-and-breakfast with a restored exterior that leaves passersby awestruck, Grandmere's has a scant six rooms. It is amazing what can be done with six rooms. Each features a four-poster queen bed, private bath, and access to some of the most beautiful grounds around. Frequently featured in the Spring Home and Garden Tour, the lush lawns and groomed gardens of Grandmere's are often used as the backdrop to wedding ceremonies. Picturesque to say the least. Morning brings a hefty helping of scones, French toast, quiche, and other elegantly nostalgic breakfast foods. $$$. (530) 265-4660.

**The Emma Nevada House.** 528 East Broad Street, Nevada City, CA 95959. Named for a nineteenth-century opera star who hailed from Nevada City, this B&B has quirky details that make it a fun getaway. There is an antique slot machine in the game room, claw-foot and Jacuzzi tubs in the baths, and a room called Emma's Hide-away, with two attic hideaway nooks. Without compromising the historical beauty of the home, The Emma Nevada House staff remembers that a stay here is a retreat and gets you excited about having a name for your room rather than a number. Full breakfast in Dining Room or Sun Room when you awaken. $$$. (800) 916-3662.

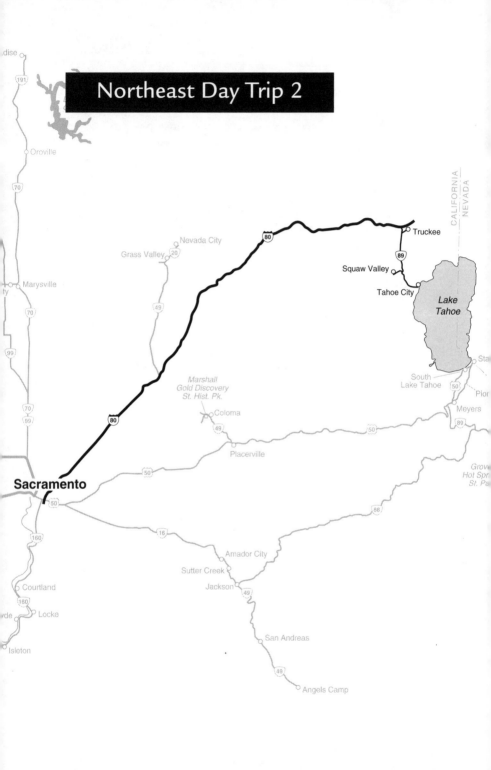

## NORTHEAST DAY TRIP 2

### Truckee
### North Lake Tahoe

About a half hour east of Sacramento, I–80 begins rising gently up into the foothills of the Sierra Nevada, and forty-five minutes later you're into some serious mountain scenery. Mammoth granite peaks—some with snow on them year-round—rise dramatically above the timberline, and deep-blue alpine lakes lie nestled in bowls carved by glaciers 10,000 years ago. Donner Summit is the high point on the route, at 7,239 feet, as well as the dividing point of this part of the Sierras. Once over the top, you drop steeply down into the Lake Tahoe Basin, a wonderland of beauty and recreation, including some of the best winter-sports opportunities in the world—Squaw Valley, between Tahoe City and Truckee, was the site of the 1960 Winter Olympics.

As you drive over the pass, try to imagine the plight of the Donner Party, who set out from Springfield, Illinois, in April of 1846, bound for the bounty of California. Having heard of a shorter and supposedly easier route, the original party split from the main party, and eighty-seven members, led by George Donner, cut south, hoping to make it over the pass before winter rolled in. It might have, had they been more familiar with the route, but the "shortcut" ended up taking them even longer, and an October storm caught them northwest of Lake Tahoe, near where I–80 now passes. And there they stayed, trapped, holed up in snow caves, their numbers dwindling with the killing cold. Soon, their already-low rations were exhausted, and their cattle had either been slaughtered and eaten or had wandered off and died.

By spring, forty-seven of the group had died; a handful had made the trek out alone or in small groups. The few who stayed managed to survive only by eating the flesh of their fallen compatriots.

# TRUCKEE

Named for a Paiute Indian, Tro-kay, who befriended an immigrant party, Truckee sits at the east end of beautiful Donner Lake, 14 miles northwest of Lake Tahoe. At one time a bustling lumber and railroad town, Truckee is now best known for its proximity to a great variety of year-round recreational opportunities. Much of old-town Truckee has been reconstructed, and Commercial Row, as it's now called, is lined with tourist-oriented gift shops, restaurants, boutiques, and real-estate offices, as well as the occasional locals' tavern.

## WHERE TO GO

A good place to start is the **Chamber of Commerce Visitor Center** in the old train depot, 10065 Donner Pass Road, directly across the street from Commercial Row. Here you can pick up maps, brochures, and other literature on the area, as well as menu guides and directories for historical walking tours. Free parking is available just east of the center.

**Donner Memorial State Park.** Donner Pass Road, Truckee, CA 96161. This 350-acre park, located just off I-80 at the east end of Donner Lake, includes both recreational facilities and the Immigrant Trail Museum, which offers an excellent chance to learn the fascinating and terrible details of the ill-fated Donner Party. In addition to viewing artifacts discovered at the site and viewing slide shows and videos depicting the group's ordeal, you can walk out onto the grounds to the exact sites of the snow caves and makeshift cabins where the members holed up during the winter of 1846–47. There are also other exhibits featuring the area's other history, particularly the railroad and logging industries. Recreational facilities include camping, picnicking, fishing, and boating.

The park is open daily Memorial Day through mid-October. The museum is open daily year-round. Small admission fee to each. (530) 582-7892.

## WHERE TO SHOP

Although Truckee touts its small mall of **factory stores** (Big Dogs, Reebok, etc.), Truckee's best place to shop is **Mountain Valley True**

**Value Hardware.** This is a classic small-town store that sells just about anything you can possibly imagine needing for outdoor sports or work, as well as for indoor enterprises. Whether you're looking for a fishing pole or frying pan, Frisbee or freeze-dried fettuccini, you'll find it here. Plus, the folks who work here are far friendlier and more helpful than they have any right to be, considering how crazy the place gets in the height of the tourist season, when Dad needs a fishing license, Mom's looking for hiking boots, and the kids want an inflatable raft for the lake. Bonus: There's an espresso stand right outside the front door! The store is located at Donner Pass Road and I–80. (530) 587–4844.

You'll also want to spend some time poking into the shops on **Commercial Row.** Here, you'll find boutiques and specialty shops, as well as the requisite T-shirt and I-heart-Truckee-mug stores.

## WHERE TO EAT

**Coffee And.** Commercial Row, Truckee, CA 96160. This little coffee shop and diner is a veritable Truckee tradition, having served locals and tourists alike for decades. Breakfast specialties include omelets and pancakes, while burgers and soups are featured on the lunch menu. Open for breakfast and lunch daily. $. (530) 587–3123.

**O.B.'s Pub and Restaurant.** Commercial Row, Truckee, CA 96160. Another longstanding local favorite, O.B.'s serves lunch and dinner daily, with entrees ranging from fish and chips to salads, pastas, prime rib, and catch-of-the-day fish specials. A comfortable atmosphere and cozy interior—decorated with historic photos of the area—make for a pleasant evening's meal after a day skiing or exploring the north-shore area. $–$$. (530) 587–4164.

## WHERE TO STAY

**Truckee Hotel.** 10007 Bridge Street, Truckee, CA 96160. Located on the corner of Bridge (Commercial Row) and Donner Pass Road, this hotel, which dates from the early 1870s, offers history and convenience. Completely renovated in 1993, the hotel has a gorgeously appointed first-floor parlor and dining room, while the guest rooms are upstairs. Rooms vary in size, some sleeping up to six. Some of the rooms have private baths. Continental breakfast included. $$. (530) 587–4444.

**Best Western Truckee Tahoe Inn.** 11331 Highway 267, Truckee, CA 96161. More than a hundred rooms are available in this motel, as well as whirlpools and spas for that after-ski soak. $$-$$$. (530) 587-4525.

## NORTH LAKE TAHOE

Stretching from the California-Nevada state line to Tahoe City, Lake Tahoe's north shore offers stunning views of the lake and surrounding mountains and nearly unlimited recreational possibilities—from tennis and golf at private resorts to camping and swimming at public beaches. Just a drive along the shoreline is impressive. You'll see brand-new homes clinging to cliffsides—boats anchored just off their back decks—as well as rustic lodges dating from the mid-twentieth century. And if you look real hard, through the pines and sometimes through iron gates, you can catch glimpses of huge waterfront estates, many with 5,000-square-foot homes as well as outbuildings that formerly served as housing for the "help."

### WHERE TO GO

**North Lake Tahoe Resort Association.** 245 North Lake Boulevard, Tahoe City, CA 96145. Operating as a visitor-information source, this association can provide lots of information on lodging, dining, activities, and events in the area. (530) 581-6900.

**Tahoe City.** Allow yourself at least a couple of hours to explore the shops of Tahoe City. A hub of both winter and summer sports, this little town has a disproportionate number of outdoor-oriented stores, specializing in skiing (snow and water), mountain biking, fishing, hiking, and just about anything you can do outside in the mountains. At the east end of town, there's a "mall" of sorts, an airy and pleasant two-story building with a toy store, a women's boutique, and a men's store with some of the coolest Hawaiian shirts this side of Lahaina.

Be sure to check out **Fanny Bridge,** where Lake Tahoe spills out into the Truckee River at the junction of CA-89 and CA-28. Named for the omnipresent rear ends lined up along the bridge—their owners bent over looking at the monstrous trout (fishing is not allowed) feeding in the swirling water below—Fanny Bridge is a Tahoe City institution. During summer you can join the thousands who spend a lazy three hours rafting from Fanny Bridge to River Ranch. Launch your own raft from the park on the south shore or rent a commercial raft from one of the many companies on the stream's north side, including **Fanny Bridge Rafts** at (530) 581-0123. Return shuttle is included in the price of raft rental (about $20, with discounts for kids).

**Squaw Valley.** This huge ski area, whose lifts and runs sprawl over several mountainsides midway between Tahoe City and Truckee, was put on the international map forty years ago when it was chosen as the site of the 1960 Winter Olympics. California skiing was still in its infancy then, and few in the ski industry thought Squaw had a chance of being selected. Since that time Squaw Valley has developed into one of the best ski resorts anywhere, attracting winter-sports enthusiasts from around the globe. The resort has targeted summer visitors as well, and on most days from late May through early September, the valley buzzes with golfers, mountain bikers, fishers, hikers, and horseback riders, as well as sightseers, who can take the tram some 2,000 feet up the mountain to spectacular views and, if they so desire, hike back down. For information on Squaw Valley activities, call (800) 545-4350. For lodging information call (800) 403-0206. For horseback tours of lower Squaw Valley, call **Squaw Valley Stables** at (530) 583-7433.

**Sugar Pine Point State Park.** Located along the northwest shore of Lake Tahoe and affording spectacular views of the lake and distant mountains, this is the largest of the basin's many state parks. Both camping and picnicking facilities are available year-round. Grab a lawn chair and the latest Tom Clancy novel and kick back on the beach; then read a paragraph or two before falling fast asleep in mountain sun or the shade of the peaceful pines. For camping reservations call (530) 525-7982. To get there go south from Tahoe City on CA-89 approximately 6 miles.

## WHERE TO EAT

**Lanza's.** 7739 North Lake Boulevard, King's Beach, CA 96143. Serving some of the best Italian food in the Tahoe Basin since the early 1930s, Lanza's is in a class by itself, and though you might have to wait for a table, especially in the height of the summer tourist season, it'll be worth your while. Entrees include pastas, veal and chicken dishes, as well as pizzas and eggplant parmigiana—plus a decent wine list, including several grades of chianti, to wash it all down with. My kids love all the dishes on the children's menu. $$. (530) 546-2434.

**Rosie's Cafe.** 571 North Lake Tahoe Boulevard, Tahoe City, CA 96145. This funky high-ceilinged and hardwood-floored restaurant, decorated with hanging plants, old skis, and other winter-sports equipment, has been serving up generous portions of good food to generations of visitors and locals alike. An excellent place to jump-start your day, Rosie's is very popular for breakfast but also serves lunch and dinner (burgers, pastas, soups, salads). Open daily. $-$$. (530) 583-1812.

**Bridgetender Tavern.** 30 West Lake Tahoe Boulevard, Tahoe City, CA 96145. Located at the Lake Tahoe-Truckee River Spillway (about three butts south of Fanny Bridge), this has been a popular hangout for generations of rowdy after-skiers and river rats. Grab a microbrew and a burger or salad and iced tea, and relax with locals who've just come in after a day operating ski lifts or shuttling rafters between Fanny Bridge and River Ranch. Open for lunch and dinner daily. $-$$. (530) 583-3342.

## WHERE TO STAY

**Lake of the Sky Motor Inn.** 955 North Lake Tahoe Boulevard, Tahoe City, CA 96145. Nothing fancy here, just a long-standing north Lake Tahoe tradition in classic A-frame style. Twenty-three rooms. Located within easy walking distance of Tahoe City shops. $$. (530) 583-3305.

**River Ranch Lodge.** Box 197, Tahoe City, CA 96145 (on CA-89 and Alpine Meadows Road). For more than a century, this lodge (rebuilt in the 1950s) has been a favorite stop for folks looking for a place to bed down, take a drink, a meal, and/or just rest beside the clear waters of the Truckee. Today it's best known as the "take-out" spot for summer river rats, who put in upstream in Tahoe City and meander down the shallow stream. In fact, several rafting companies based in Tahoe City use the turn-around at River Ranch to pick up their clients and shuttle them back to town. It's also right on the bike path that parallels the river out of Tahoe City. During winter the lodge's ideal location midway between Truckee and Tahoe City offers excellent access to local ski areas, particularly Squaw Valley and Alpine Meadows. Eighteen rooms, some with balconies overlooking the river. $$-$$$. (530) 583-4262.

**The Resort at Squaw Creek.** 400 Squaw Creek Road, Olympic Valley, CA 96146. If you're looking for upscale and fancy, this is it. This multifaceted resort features three heated pools, a golf course, a fitness center, and mountain-biking trails and rentals. During winter it offers downhill and cross-country skiing, as well as an ice rink. In addition, it's home to one of the Tahoe Basin's most elegant restaurants. $$$. (800) 327-3353.

East Day Trip 1

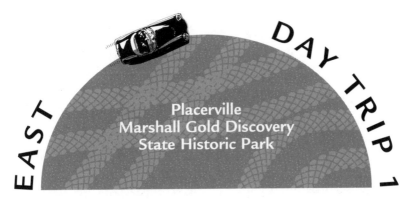

One of the best and least taxing day trips from Sacramento is one spent exploring the region just east of the city, where the foothills rise up out of the Sacramento Valley, gradually transforming into the striking granite peaks and steep precipices of the daunting Sierra Nevada. Here you can follow the paths of gold rush pioneers, who panned and sluiced and hard-rock mined—often without reward—in these parts a century and a half ago. In addition, you can visit the spot where the gold rush was launched: John Sutter's sawmill, where, in January of 1848, carpenter James Marshall discovered a few shiny specks of gold in the clear waters of the American River.

Though you're likely to encounter intriguing distractions along the way—always allow for the unexpected—the complete circle, from Sacramento to Placerville, up to Coloma and Sutter's Mill (part of Marshall Gold Discovery State Historic Park), then back to Sacramento via I-80, is less than 200 miles, a wonderful day trip, especially on an autumn day, when the leaves are changing to reds and golds, or in springtime, when wildflowers carpet the meadows and hillsides.

## PLACERVILLE

Placerville is an easy, under-an-hour drive from Sacramento, and though quite nearby, it is strikingly different in many ways. First of all, its location in the heart of the Sierra Nevada foothills provides dramatic relief from the valley floor, grassy, scrub-oak-covered hillsides having given way to sprawling stands of tall fir and pine trees.

43

This location also provides for a cooler climate, its nearly 2,000-foot elevation almost always guaranteeing temperatures ten to twenty degrees lower than those in Sacramento. Finally, Placerville's population is decidedly un-urban: Founded as a center of gold mining and trade, the town, at one time known as "Hangtown," out of respect for frontier justice, has always prided itself on existing on its own terms. Though the mid-nineteenth-century lawlessness for which the community was once famous has mostly given way to civility and decorum, and though folks from Sacramento have built spacious hillside homes here from which they commute to jobs in the city, Placerville retains an exciting, nearly palpable edge.

## WHERE TO GO

**El Dorado County Chamber of Commerce.** 542 Main Street, Placerville, CA 95667. For complete information on what to see and do, as well as on where to eat and stay in the area, stop in at the chamber's offices. Stock up on brochures and other literature. Open weekdays. On weekends there's an information booth at the train caboose, junction of Highways 49 and 50. (530) 621-5885.

**El Dorado County Historical Museum.** 104 Placerville Drive, Placerville, CA 95667. This is an excellent place to get a sense not only of Placerville's and El Dorado County's history, but of the surrounding gold country and the gold rush itself. You'll also get a sense of what else contributed to the development of the area after the relatively short-lived frenzy for the precious yellow metal. View displays documenting the region's logging, ranching, and early commerce, as well as the Pony Express, which passed through here for eighteen months from 1860 to 1861, until the telegraph put the riders out of work. (530) 621-5865.

**Gold Bug Mine.** Bedford Avenue (in Bedford Park), Placerville, CA 95667. At one time literally thousands of mines dotted the Placerville countryside, and there were hundreds within a nugget's throw of town hall. The Gold Bug, which tapped into the famous Mother Lode vein, is owned and operated by the city of Placerville and is a good place to get a feel for what it was like inside the mines during their heyday. Both guided and self-guided tours are available. Small admission fee. Open daily April through October, weekends only the rest of the year. (530) 642-5232.

## WHERE TO EAT

Lots of fast-food places for folks passing through en route to Tahoe or points farther east, but if you're into checking out the local flavor, there's plenty to choose from as well.

**Plaza Cafe and Espresso.** 3964 Missouri Flat Road, Placerville, CA 95667. Stop in here for a latte and pastry in the morning, or for lunch or picnic fixin's in the afternoon. Closed Sunday. $. (530) 642-9996.

**Li'l Mama D'Carlo's.** 482 Main Street, Placerville, CA 95667. A local favorite for Italian, this downtown restaurant specializes in southern-Italian food, including pastas, seafood, and veal dishes. Open for dinner Wednesday through Sunday. $$. (530) 626-1612.

## WHERE TO STAY

Many of Placerville's hillside Victorian homes have been converted to bed-and-breakfasts, with meticulous restoration and authentic furnishings providing true Queen Anne charm. Among them:

**The Shafksy House.** 2942 Coloma Street, Placerville, CA 95667. Three beautifully appointed rooms are available in this 1902 home, each with private bath. $$$. (530) 642-2772.

**The Combellack-Blair House.** 3059 Cedar Ravine Road, Placerville, CA 95667. A highlight here is the gorgeous spiral staircase, as well as beautiful landscaping. House dates from 1895. Four rooms, all with private baths. $$$. (530) 622-3764.

**The Seasons Bed and Breakfast.** 2934 Bedford Avenue, Placerville, CA 95667. Among the city's oldest homes (1859) and at one time a gold-stamp mill, this small inn offers three guest rooms and a separate cabin. $$$. (530) 626-4420.

For motel accommodations try the following:

**Mother Lode Motel.** 1940 Broadway, Placerville, CA 95667. Small (twenty-one rooms) and basic, but clean and dependable motel accommodations. $-$$. (530) 622-0895.

**Best Western Placerville Inn.** 6850 Greenleaf Court, Placerville, CA 95667. Some of the one-hundred-plus rooms have fireplaces, and suites are available. $$. (530) 622-9100.

For Placerville central reservations call **Gold Country Lodging** at (877) 262-4667.

# MARSHALL GOLD DISCOVERY STATE HISTORIC PARK

Although gold would have eventually been discovered by someone somewhere in the Sierra Nevada foothills, and the gold rush would have just as surely occurred as soon as word spread, chance dictated that it happened here, near Coloma on the American River. In 1847 James Marshall, a carpenter in the employ of Sacramento businessman John Sutter, was sent upriver to build a sawmill for his boss. One day in January of the following year, the mill nearly completed, Marshall happened to look down into the shallow waters of the river's edge, and, there, lo and behold, were some shiny yellow flecks on the streambed.

Gold.

Marshall took his find to Sutter's office in Sacramento and announced his find. Within six months, some 4,000 miners were working the river—both up- and downstream from the mill—hoping to cash in on Marshall's discovery. Soon men were streaming into the northern California foothills from every corner of the globe. By 1852 an estimated 100,000 men—some of whom had come overland across the plains and over the Rocky Mountains, some of whom had come by ship around Cape Horn to San Francisco Bay, where ships sat abandoned in harbor—were hardscrabbling the foothills in search of fortune. And though a few did strike it rich, by far the larger percentage returned home broke or settled in California at other pursuits, such as ranching or farming. Marshall and Sutter themselves both died bitter and penniless.

At 280-acre **Marshall Gold Discovery State Historic Park** you can visit James Marshall's cabin and a replica of the mill he built for John Sutter. There's also a museum with exhibits explicating gold-mining techniques, as well as displays honoring native Americans of the area (Maidu), who were mostly trampled over and forgotten by the gold-hungry forty-niners and those who came after them. The park and museum are open daily, with small per-vehicle (park) and individual (museum) admission fees. Picnic facilities are available in the shade along the river. (530) 622-3470 (park); (530) 622-1116 (museum).

To get to the park from Placerville, take CA-49 north about 8 miles and watch for the signs (the highway number is no coincidence, nor are the shovel-shaped highway markers). You can return to Sacramento the way you came or continue north on CA-49 to I-80, where you can go west and head back into Sacramento through Auburn, Rocklin, and Roseville.

## WHERE TO STAY

**Coloma Country Inn.** 345 High Street, Box 502, Coloma, CA 95613. Seven rooms are available in this bed-and-breakfast located on five acres within the state historic park. Five of the rooms are in the main house, built in 1852, while two larger suites are in an adjoining carriage house, dating from 1898. The innkeepers specialize in arranging adventure outings in the area—from white-water rafting to hot-air ballooning, but even if you're not interested in such things, this is an ideally located "base camp" from which to explore the region. $$. (530) 622-6919.

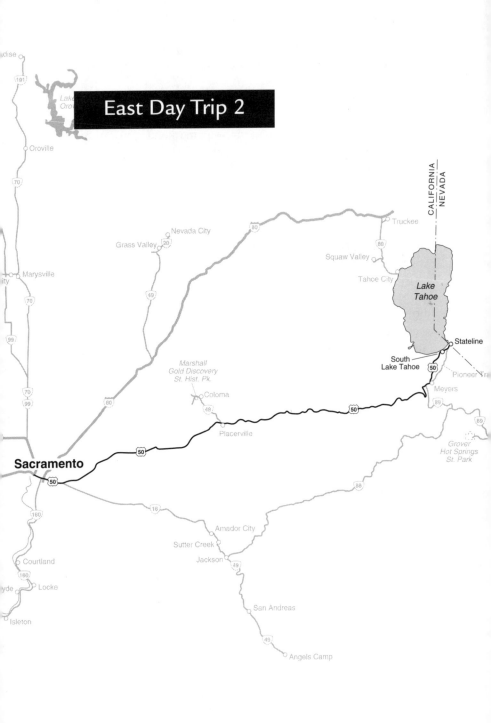

# SOUTH LAKE TAHOE

South Lake Tahoe is an easy two-hour drive from Sacramento, though during winter, new snow on Highway 50's Echo Summit (7,382 feet) can slow the trip down considerably. Road restrictions are often in effect, mandating snow chains and/or four-wheel-drive vehicles only, though usually not for long, as the road is plowed as quickly as possible. Generally, during a severe storm, however, I-80 to north shore and on to Reno will be plowed before Highway 50 to south shore, as it's the more widely traveled east-west route over the mountains.

Keep in mind also that traffic can be downright nasty once you drop down into the Tahoe Basin and approach South Lake Tahoe. Weekends year-round, as well as most summer days, traffic is often backed up by early afternoon from the junction of Highway 50 and CA-89 clear to Stateline. For road conditions call (800) 472-ROAD.

## WHERE TO GO

**South Lake Tahoe Chamber of Commerce.** 3066 Lake Tahoe Boulevard, South Lake Tahoe, CA 96150. This is a good place to stop before entering into the craziness of Stateline or venturing out to the state parks or other outdoor attractions. Pick up maps and brochures, and get advice on what's happening in the area. (530) 521-5255.

**Lake Tahoe Visitors Center.** Operated by the U.S. Forest Service and located in a gorgeously scenic site on the southwest shore of the lake, this little visitor center on Taylor Creek will provide an overview of the history, flora, fauna, and environmental issues in and around the lake. To get there go north on CA–89 at the "Y" (the junction of Highway 50 and CA–89, and watch for the signs on the east (lake) side of the road.

**Emerald Bay/Vikingsholm.** Continue north along CA–89 as it hugs the west shore of Lake Tahoe and passes through lush meadows and shadowy fir and sugar-pine forests. Emerald Bay is a thumb-shaped crystalline inlet on the lake's southwest shore, the prettiest part of one of the prettiest places on the planet. Parking is limited, especially on summer afternoons, but if you can grab a spot in either the Emerald Bay or Eagle Falls parking lot (there are also pull-outs along the road near the designated lots), you'll want to grab your camera and take advantage of the photo op. On clear summer days you won't find a more striking vista than the blue-green jewel of a bay with its tiny stone island foregrounding the pale blue lake behind it, the deep green mountains that surround it, and the sky, maybe brushed with wisps of high clouds.

If you feel like a little exercise, take the short half-mile hike up to Eagle Falls, or continue on another mile or so to Eagle Lake. Up here, even if the parking lot's packed and the traffic on the main road is backed up, you'll find yourself nearly alone in the quiet of the forest. Picnic facilities and rest rooms are located at the parking lot; day-use fee is $3.00 per car.

Another excellent way to explore the Emerald Bay area is to hike down to Vikingsholm, a thirty-eight-room summer home built in 1928 and modeled after a medieval Scandinavian castle. The stone structure on the island in the middle of the bay was where the home's owner took her tea in the afternoons. Located right on the shore of Emerald Bay, Vikingsholm is open to the public for tours June through August (small admission fee). There are also picnic tables, although neither food nor water is available. The hike is an easy one, a mile down a gravel service road, which switches back several times to accommodate the steepness of the mountainside.

For information on Emerald Bay State Park, call (530) 998–0205. For information on Vikingsholm call (530) 525–7277.

**Heavenly Valley.** Ski Run Boulevard, South Lake Tahoe, CA 96151. Even if you're not a skier—or even if it's the middle of summer—check out this ski resort rising steeply above the casinos and high-rise chaos of South Lake Tahoe. Sight-seeing tram rides

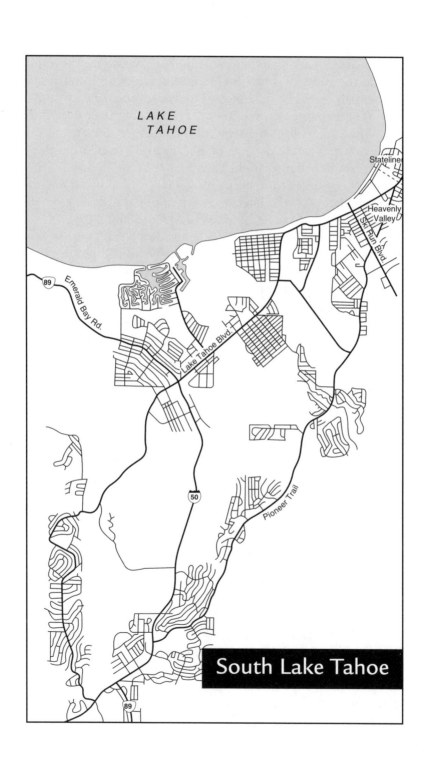

LAKE
TAHOE

Stateline

Heavenly
Ski Run Blvd.
Valley

89

Emerald Bay Rd.

Lake Tahoe Blvd.

50

Pioneer Trail

89

**South Lake Tahoe**

from the base (parking lot) are available both during the ski season and during summer, when the restaurant serves both lunch and dinner daily. You'd be hard-pressed to find a better view than that from the deck at the top of the tram, 2,000 feet above lake level. Once you've had your fill of the view and/or lunch or dinner, you can either ride the tram back down or hike down. Tram rides are about $12 for adults, half price for kids.

Skiers can explore the mountain's 4,800 acres and two states; the resort straddles the state line, so you can ride up the chairlift in California and ski down to lunch in Nevada. (775) 586-7000.

**The Casinos.** If you've never been inside a Nevada casino, you owe it to yourself to wander through one, even if you don't plan to gamble. Watch the blue-rinse crowd feeding nickels into the slot machines—sometimes three machines at a time. Check out the high rollers at the blackjack tables and roulette wheels. Though the really big-money betting is done in roped-off areas, you can watch over the shoulders of bettors at $5.00-to-$25.00-minimum tables, putting perhaps as much as $1,000 on a single blackjack hand.

And though you'll be tempted to place a bet or two yourself, keep in mind that the odds are decidedly in the casinos' favor: They haven't built these luxury casinos by taking losses. Remember, too, that generally the simpler the game, the worse the odds; the slot machines, offering the easiest bets to make, also offer the worst odds in the house. Keep in mind, too, that the "free" drinks offered to gamblers are often anything but—when you consider you'll most likely drop $20 while you're nursing it.

One true bargain in the casinos is the buffet dinners, where you can get decent food—and lots of it—at very reasonable prices (see Where to Eat section). Note, though, how the line to get in passes right past the slot machines. Try to avoid joining the very large percentage of folks who get good deals on dinner and then drop another $30 or $40 either on their way in or out, or both.

Harvey's and Harrah's are the two largest casinos in South Lake Tahoe and are across the street from each other, just over the state line in Nevada. Parking is "free." Some of the smaller casinos on the east end of town offer smaller minimum bets and a more relaxed atmosphere. The casinos are open twenty-four hours a day seven days a week.

**Lake Cruises.** There's nothing quite like actually being out on the water on Lake Tahoe, whether you're looking out at the surrounding mountains or deep into the crystalline water, or just enjoying the cool spray splashing up from the boat's bow. Take advantage of any opportunity to go out on the lake in a private boat, and if you can't do that, several companies offer sight-seeing tours of the lake, which might be the next-best thing. The **MS** *Dixie II* (775-588-3508) and the *Tahoe Queen* (530-541-3364) are both large paddle wheelers offering a variety of tours: champagne breakfast, sunset dinner, and Emerald Bay sight-seeing, as well as private charters. Prices start at about $16 for a half-day cruise and vary according to length of trip.

## WHERE TO EAT

**Red Hut Cafe.** 2749 Lake Tahoe Boulevard, South Lake Tahoe, CA 96150. Without a doubt one of the best breakfast places in the state, the Red Hut is a virtual institution in Tahoe. Be prepared to wait, however, as it's no secret that this little place serves some of the best waffles, omelets, and other breakfast grub in the basin. Open for breakfast and lunch daily. $-$$. (530) 541-9024. There's also a Red Hut at 219 Kingsbury in Stateline. (775) 588-2626.

**Sprouts Natural Foods Cafe.** 3123 Harrison (corner of Lake Tahoe Boulevard), South Lake Tahoe, CA 96150. This popular health-food restaurant is a welcome respite from the fast-paced and high-rolling lifestyle that defines much of South Lake Tahoe. Serving breakfast, lunch, and dinner daily, Sprouts specializes in fresh-squeezed juices, muffins, smoothies, soups, salads, and healthful sandwiches (from tuna to turkey to tempeh). $-$$. (530) 541-6969.

**Cantina Bar and Grill.** 765 Emerald Bay Road, South Lake Tahoe, CA 95161. Longtime regulars will remember this good-time Mexican restaurant as Cantina de los Tres Hombres, which served the south-shore area for more than twenty years. Today, under new ownership, the restaurant is still a popular watering hole and place to munch nachos or enjoy a multicourse dinner, ranging from tacos to tamales, burritos to buñuelos. $$. (530) 544-1233.

The buffets in the casinos offer excellent deals on food, and the quality is generally quite good. Just watch your wallet: Your $14.95 dinner can easily cost you $60.00 or more if you stop to hit the slots or the blackjack tables on your way out. The two best buffets

in town are **The Garden Buffet,** in Harvey's Resort Hotel at Stateline (775-588-2411), and **Friday's Station,** in Harrah's Tahoe
(775-588-6611). Weekday prices are about $15 for all you can eat;
on weekends, when the buffets include prime rib and fresh seafood
prices are about $20.

**Nephele's.** 1169 Ski Boulevard, South Lake Tahoe, CA 96150. For
an upper-end treat, try this longtime favorite, whose specials include
pastas, beef, and regular seafood specials. $$$. (530) 544-8130.

**Fresh Ketch.** 2435 Venice Drive, South Lake Tahoe, CA 96151.
Though a good four-hour drive from the ocean, this popular seafood
restaurant—located on the lake overlooking the water and marina at
Tahoe Keys—serves excellent salmon, crab, ahi, and various other
fresh seafood and shellfish, depending on the season and the
weather. Diners with aversions to seafood can choose from beef,
chicken, salads, and other regular entrees as well as daily specials.
Open daily for dinner. $$$. (530) 544-5683.

## WHERE TO STAY

You'll find a huge range of places to stay in Tahoe, from ski-in
condos on the slopes of Heavenly Valley and lush rooms in the high-
rise casinos to tacky motels with weekly and monthly (and probably
even hourly) rates. No matter your preference, however, you'd be ill
advised to show up without reservations, especially in summer and
on weekends during the ski season.

**Harvey's Resort Hotel and Casino.** Box 128, Stateline, NV
89449. Rooms in the heart of the madness of south shore, where a
blackjack table or a slot machine is just a hallway and an elevator
ride away. Prices range depending on season and amenities; during
the off-season, Harvey's and many of the other casinos offer
reduced-price incentive packages. $$$. (775) 588-7777.

**Lakeland Village Beach and Ski Resort.** 3535 Lake Tahoe
Boulevard, South Lake Tahoe, CA 96150. A confession: Lakeland
Village has been a personal favorite of mine since the early 1970s,
when I was a lowly lift operator at Heavenly Valley and my buddies
and I would all head down to this upscale lodge and sneak into the
spa. Very nice outdoor Jacuzzi and private beach. Rates range
depending on the number of people in your room(s), which are
equipped with kitchens. $$$. (530) 544-1685.

**Holiday Inn Express.** 3961 Lake Tahoe Boulevard, South Lake Tahoe, CA 96150. Convenience and cleanliness, if not a whole lot of character, at Holiday Inn's restaurant-less hotels. $$. (800) 288-2463.

**Fantasy Inn and Wedding Chapel.** 3696 Lake Tahoe Boulevard, South Lake Tahoe, CA 96150. Hey, why not? Waveless water beds, mirrored ceilings, showers for two, adult movies, in-room heart-shaped spas . . . the Fantasy Inn offers all this and more. Ski packages, wedding and honeymoon services, and theme suites are also available. Try Graceland, Romeo and Juliet, Rain Forest, and, er, Queen's Quarters. $$$. (800) 367-7736.

**Super 8 Motel.** 3600 Lake Tahoe Boulevard, South Lake Tahoe, CA 96150. For something a little more generic. $$. (530) 544-3476.

**Heavenly Tahoe Vacations.** Box 2180, Stateline, NV 89449. This is a Heavenly Valley–based central-reservation service with links to scores of lodging options in the South Lake Tahoe area. (775) 586-7050 or (800) 243-2836; www. skiheavenly.com.

Southeast Day Trip 1

Lake Oroville

Oroville

99

70

Nevada City

Grass Valley    20

80    Squaw Valley

utter
ttes

Marysville

Yuba City

70

49

Tah

99

70
99

Marshall
Gold Discovery
St. Hist. Pk.

Coloma

80

49

50

Placerville

50

Sacramento

50

5

50

16

88

Amador City

160

Sutter Creek

Courtland

Jackson    49

160

Ryde    Locke

San Andreas

sta    Isleton

49

Angels Camp

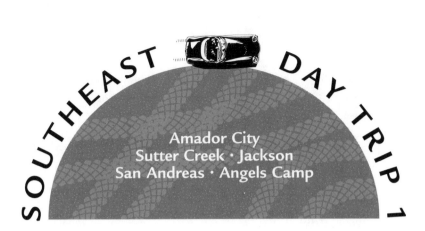

SOUTHEAST DAY TRIP 1

Amador City
Sutter Creek · Jackson
San Andreas · Angels Camp

California's central gold country is as historically fascinating as it is visually arresting. Of course, every schoolchild knows the basic story: On January 28, 1948, James Marshall, who has been building a sawmill near Coloma, strolls into the office of his Sacramento employer, John Sutter, and announces he has discovered flecks of gold in the American River near Coloma. Within months the foothills from north of Nevada City south to Sonora are crawling with miners who have flocked to the area, largely from the Midwest and East Coast. By mid-1849 San Francisco Bay is jammed with ships of every size and shape—many of which have come around Cape Horn—abandoned by their crews, young men from around the world with dreams of striking it rich in the gold fields.

And though some newcomers did get rich in the mines, or by providing much-needed services to the miners—Levi Strauss by making blue jeans, Philip Armour by providing meat—the large percentage of those who came were disappointed. Many ended up in other pursuits—ranching and farming, particularly—whereas others returned to their families. Even Marshall and Sutter rued their discovery, both dying broke.

Today, a visit to California's gold country provides a chance to visit that past. Most of the towns have pioneer museums, some with model working mines, and the narrow streets, old hotels, and Victorian homes clinging to cliffsides remind visitors of the days when the area was abuzz not only with mines but with assayers' offices, storefront banks, brothels, gambling houses, and rowdy taverns.

But more than that, the gold country offers some downright stunning scenery. The two best times of the year are in spring, when the wildflowers carpet the rolling hillsides, and in late fall, when frost lingers in morning shadows and the leaves turn to brilliant reds and golds. As charming as the little gold country towns are—with their pioneer cemeteries, gift shops, and Queen Anne-style homes converted to bed-and-breakfasts—the roads that link them can be even more stimulating. Head south on CA-49, named for the year of the miners. Wind through ancient oak forests and across broad, grassy meadows, where sheep, cattle, and horses graze peacefully. Drop down into darkened canyons and then rise up over broad knolls that offer views for miles, sometimes far into the valley to the west or up into the towering Sierra Nevada to the east. You might not see what the miners were looking for, but you just might see gold.

# AMADOR CITY

After taking CA-16 southeast from Sacramento for about 30 miles, you want to catch CA-49 south; the intersection is well marked. From here on down to Jamestown, the little two-laner winds through the heart of the gold country, passing through a dozen or so 1950s-era towns along the way, in most of which you'll find gift and souvenir shops as well as small restaurants and inns. Amador City is the first one you pass through. Like most, it has been boutiqued and gift-shopped, but it's still worth getting out of your car to wander along the boardwalk sidewalks of the 1-block length of town.

## WHERE TO GO

Most of the dozen or so little shops in Amador City are typical of those you find in all of the gold country towns, with one exception: **Red Skelton's Gallery of Clowns.** Located at 14191 CA-49, this tiny little gallery sells estate-authorized reproductions of clown paintings by Red Skelton, in addition to a variety of souvenirs: mugs, videos, calendars, and other items. Prices for framed paintings range from $200 to $400. (Apparently, the real McCoy can run to $100,000.) (209) 267-0913.

## WHERE TO EAT AND STAY

**Buffalo Chips Emporium.** 14179 CA–49, Amador City, CA 95601. This narrow little street-front diner and soda fountain serves good lunches—burgers, chile, salads—as well as ice-cream desserts. The antique wall decorations—old cigarette and Coca Cola ads—provide atmosphere as well as diversions while you wait for your food. $–$$. (209) 267-0570.

   **Imperial Hotel and Restaurant.** 14202 CA–49, Amador City, CA 95601. For a more substantial meal, try this upscale restaurant located inside the restored 1880s-era Imperial Hotel. The menu changes regularly but characteristically features California cuisine cooked with local ingredients. $$–$$$. Lodging is also available here, with six upstairs rooms decorated in period antiques. $$$. (209) 267-9172.

# SUTTER CREEK

Just a few miles south of Amador City on CA–49, Sutter Creek was the site of Leland Stanford's Lincoln Mine. Stanford invested in the railroad and went on to become one of early California's richest and most influential people. Like Amador City, Sutter Creek is built in a little hollow, the road dropping down into town, then doglegging back up the hillside. Lots of gift shops, galleries, and boutiques here, favorites of late-November and December shoppers, who pack the sidewalks and little stores looking for holiday gifts, particularly Christmas ornaments and knickknacks.

## WHERE TO GO

**Sutter Creek Visitor Information.** 40 Main Street, Box 600, Sutter Creek, CA 95685. Pick up brochures detailing historical structures, local shops and eateries, as well as maps with self-guided walking tours. (209) 267-1344.

   **Volcano.** Unlike most of the gold rush towns along CA–49, where the historical buildings often house boutiques and tacky gift shops, Volcano, a bit off the beaten path, has managed to maintain a good share of its authenticity and integrity. Take CA–88 east from Sutter

Creek to this little town, founded in the early 1850s, which in the past was home to nearly twenty hotels, two theaters, a handful of dance halls, three breweries, and a law school. The **St. George Hotel** (209-296-4458), the only hotel remaining, offers rooms in the historical main building as well as in an adjoining addition, and breakfast, lunch, and dinner are served in the hotel's dining room. In spring check out four-acre **Daffodil Hill,** where some 300,000 daffodils (more than 300 varieties) and other bulbs brighten the hillside mid-March through mid-April. For specifics or to see if the hill's in bloom, call the Amador County Chamber of Commerce at (209) 223-0350.

## WHERE TO EAT

**Zinfandel's.** 51 Hanford Street, Sutter Creek, CA 95685. One of the nicest restaurants in the gold country, Zinfandel's specializes in inventive California cuisine, largely vegetarian, but with seafood, beef, and chicken dinners also available. $$-$$$. (209) 267-5008.

## WHERE TO STAY

**Grey Gables Bed and Breakfast Inn.** 161 Hanford Street, Box 1687, Sutter Creek, CA 95685. Eight rooms in a large inn located on the north end of town right along CA-49 offer convenience and comfort. The theme is "merrie olde" England here, with rooms named for British writers (my wife of Bath loved the tubs), English teas served every afternoon, and English-style breakfasts dished up each morning. $$-$$$. (209) 267-1039.

**Sutter Creek Inn.** 75 Main Street, Sutter Creek, CA 95685. We stayed here some fifteen years ago, long before bed-and-breakfasts were the rage in tourist towns around the country, and had a great time—we've gone back several times. The location couldn't be better. Walk out the front door of the main house, through the garden, and out the gate, and you're in the middle of 3-block downtown Sutter Creek. Plus, the rooms are fun, decorated less pretentiously than in some bed-and-breakfasts and—except for three, in the main house—are located about the property in various outbuildings, including a carriage house. Swingers will enjoy the hanging beds in some of the rooms. Guests always remember proprietor Jane Way's way: Breakfast right at nine, introduce yourself, and dig in. $$-$$$. (209) 267-5606.

## JACKSON

Unlike many of California's Gold Rush communities, whose booms were short-lived and which soon were mostly abandoned, Jackson has managed to maintain its bustle and sense of community since its founding in the early 1850s as a hub and supply center for placer and hardrock miners staking out the surrounding countryside. Almost completely destroyed by fire in 1862, the town was rebuilt shortly after. In 1922 forty-seven miners lost their lives in a fire deep within the Argonaut Mine. Well known even into the middle of the twentieth century as a mecca for its brothels and gambling halls—and the last town in California to outlaw prostitution—Jackson still prides itself on its frontier image, with hard-core taverns and lowball card halls sandwiched between gift shops and boutiques on Main Street. And that bustle lives on. The little town bustles so much that parking can be a downright nightmare. We were there on a recent Friday after Thanksgiving, and not only was there no parking on the street, but the public lots were full. We checked into our motel and walked into town.

### WHERE TO GO

**Amador County Chamber of Commerce.** 125 Peek Street, Jackson, CA 95642. As is usually the case, the chamber is a good place to begin a tour of the area. You'll find plenty of brochures and maps and other literature offering everything from advice on lodging and sight-seeing to coupons for two-for-one pizza and discounts on cross-country ski rental. (209) 223-0350.

    **National Hotel.** 2 Water Street, Jackson, CA 95642. Located at the south end of Main Street, this hotel has been in continuous operation for more than a century and has hosted Leland Stanford, John Wayne, and many other well-known folks. There might be better places to stay nearby these days, but you ought at least to poke your head inside. The bar must look the way it did a hundred years ago, with the dark oak walls, chandeliers, and grand piano among the tables, not to mention the cloud of smoke that hangs throughout the room, despite California's ordinances against smoking in public places. (209) 223-0500.

    **Amador County Museum.** 225 Church Street, Jackson, CA 95642. With exhibits that include a working stamp mill, a tailing mill, and a scale model of the once-productive Kennedy Mine, this museum offers an excellent overview of the history of the gold rush and the many ways the ore was extracted.

Each of the dozen or so rooms, including those at the top of a narrow, winding staircase, is devoted to displaying a certain theme, from education and fashion to mining and ranching. Open Wednesday through Sunday, with tours offered on weekends. Small admission fee. (209) 223-6386.

This particular museum made quite an impression on my eight-year-old daughter, Gina. Here's her take on it:

"The best museum in Jackson is called The Amador County Museum. The museum has lots of old-fashioned days stuff that shows us about war, school, clothes, and other things.

"School in the old days was very different than it is now. There was a really pretty dunce cap on top of the piano with stars and moons on it. I thought it was good until I heard what it was for, which was sending kids over to the corner and putting the dunce cap on for a time-out. There was also a teacher's bell in a little classroom with two little desks.

"I saw real army stuff: guns, swords, and a shield, and army hats they used in the war.

"There was a beautiful old wedding dress. It was lacy white with a lacy veil. I saw a funeral dress, just like the wedding dress except it was black. I saw one of those corsets that they used in the olden days. When the ladies wanted to be pretty and not look fat they wore the corsets, but it was bad for their lungs. I saw very pretty porcelain dolls with beautiful velvet dresses on. I also saw old baseball uniforms and a fancy old hat.

"Some of the other things I liked were old wood carriages and servants' steps—those really steep steps that servants had to go up and down with dishes. There were also some neat baskets that the Indians weaved, an Ediphone (sort of like a telephone), an old grandfather clock, a bear trap, and lots of other cool stuff. This museum is very good for kids because it has lots of interesting stuff."

**Kennedy Tailing Wheels Park.** Located just north of town on Jackson Gate Road (off Main Street; watch for the sign), this park is the site of two of the area's deepest (6,000 feet) and most productive mines, the Kennedy and the Argonaut, which were in operation until World War II. Though not open for tours, the mines do offer close-up views of their tailing wheels and head frames and provide a sense of the size of mining's contribution to the settling of this area.

## WHERE TO SHOP

Jackson's main drag is lined with gift shops, boutiques, and galleries catering to the many tourists who flock to town, and it's fun just to wander through them. Two of the most interesting stores in Jackson, however, deserve special mention.

**Amador Fireside Center.** 155 Main Street, Jackson, CA 95642. This is sort of an upscale hardware store specializing in kitchen stoves and wood-burning heating stoves. In addition, you'll find large assortments of fireplace accessories, weather vanes, and area rugs. A fun store to poke around in, particularly on a wet winter day. (209) 223-3806.

**Hein & Co. Bookstore.** 204 Main Street, Jackson, CA 95642. This is one of California's best bookstores. Selling used and rare books, as well as prints, and a few new books about the West, Hein & Co. beckons the bibliophile with aisle after aisle of books on every topic imaginable, from aviation to bullfighting to women's studies. Pick up a complete set of the *Encyclopaedia Britannica,* a set of Dickens's novels, or fill up a shopping bag with books from the large room where every book costs $1.00. The shop's strong suit is, naturally, the history of the west, and in addition to the new books you can also pick up histories dating from the early twentieth century and before. (209) 223-9076.

## WHERE TO EAT

**Mel's Diner.** 205 CA–49, Jackson, CA 95642. A classic in the true American roadside-diner tradition, Mel's has been a favorite of locals and travelers for decades, remaining virtually unchanged since 1956. Grab a stool at the counter or at a table in the bustling dining room and dig into one of Mel's huge omelets, a burger and fries, or a steak sandwich; on Fridays Mel's offers a New England clam chowder that's quite respectable given the distance from the ocean. Not for diners looking for the latest in California cuisine or the "presentation," Mel's just offers good down-home food and lots of it. Open daily for breakfast, lunch, and dinner. No credit cards. $-$$. (209) 223-0853.

**Rosebud's Classic Cafe.** 26 Main Street, Jackson, CA 95642. Another traditional all-American cafe, Rosebud's serves breakfast and lunch daily from its cozy little storefront location on Main Street, where the tables by the huge windows are perfect for watching the rest of the world wander by. No credit cards. $-$$. (209) 223-1035.

**Upstairs Restaurant and Streetside Bistro.** 164 Main Street, Jackson, CA 95642. Offering a decidedly more upscale menu than Rosebud's or Mel's, the Fireside might be a better bet if you've a romantic evening in mind or simply want to linger over your meal. Menu changes regularly, but you can count on pastas, salads, a variety of fowl, and lots of herbs. The bistro downstairs serves lunch Tuesday through Sunday, while the tiny restaurant upstairs serves dinner daily. $$-$$$. (209) 223-3342.

**Fat Freddy's.** 4 Main Street, Jackson, CA 95642. A classic soda fountain, complete with creaky screen door, located in the historic Wells Fargo building. This cozy little place serves ice-cream dishes, burgers, corn dogs, and fries, as well as frozen yogurt and chile. Perfect for filling your tummy's empty spot in mid-afternoon or for satisfying the kids' pleas for treats. $. (209) 223-2525.

### WHERE TO STAY

**Court Street Inn.** 215 Court Street, Jackson, CA 95642.  This bed-and-breakfast in an 1870s era home offers privacy and intimacy in individually decorated rooms in the main house as well as a separate cottage for up to four guests. Fireplaces and spas in some rooms. $$$. (209) 223-0416.

**Best Western Amador Inn.** 200 South CA-49, Jackson, CA 95642. Though lacking the flavor of the area's many bed-and-breakfasts, the motel is considerably less expensive and is located within walking distance of the historical downtown area. Some of the 118 rooms have kitchenettes, some fireplaces. $$.  (209) 223-0211.

## SAN ANDREAS

Though the names of vast numbers of California towns and communities—from San Diego to Monterey to Chico—reflect their Spanish-Mexican foundings, those names are far less common in the gold country. This little town, however, was settled largely by Mexican immigrants, who, in 1848, were among the gold rush's first wave of fortune seekers. In 1852 they built a small wood-frame-and-canvas church, which they named for San Andreas (St. Andrew), and thus the town took its name. That same year, a gold nugget worth $12,000 was unearthed in a mine north of town, and by 1859 gold dust worth a half a million dollars was being shipped annually from San Andreas. In 1866 San Andreas became the seat of Calaveras County.

## WHERE TO GO

**Calaveras County Museum Complex.** 30 North Main (CA–49), San Andreas, CA 95249. Located in the town's historic jail and courthouse, this museum displays artifacts from the area's history, including Native American basketry and mining relics. In addition, you can view the jail cell that held the notorious stagecoach robber Black Bart, often called the "Gentlemen Bandit" for his reputation of robbing only the very well-to-do, never hurting any of his victims, and leaving snippets of original poetry at the scenes of the crimes. After a "long and successful career," he was finally captured in 1883 and sentenced to six years in San Quentin. The museum also houses the county's archives and other historical records, many of which are available to the public, and also serves as San Andreas's visitor-information center, with brochures on things to see and do in the area. Open daily. (209) 754-6513.

    **California Caverns.** Cave City Road, off Mountain Ranch Road, 8 miles east of San Andreas. Under much of Calaveras are long, labyrinthine caves, some of which are open to the public. California Caverns, discovered in 1849 and open for limited public exploration since 1850, includes large underground "rooms," lakes, and eerie formations of stalagmites and stalactites, as well as the signatures of spelunkers who explored the cave in the nineteenth century, without the benefits of electric lighting. Self-guided and guided tours are both available. (209) 736-2708.

## WHERE TO EAT

**B of A Cafe.** 1262 South Main, San Andreas, CA 95249. Located in the restored 1936-vintage Bank of America building (hence, the name) and decorated with Depression-era banking artifacts, the B of A Cafe specializes in California-cuisine lunches—greens, healthful breads, pastas—and hearty dinners, including a Sunday-night Basque, family-style special, including lamb, chicken, and steak. It also stocks a wide assortment of wines from local wineries. Open daily for lunch, and Thursday through Sunday for dinner. $$–$$$. (209) 736–0765.

## WHERE TO STAY

**Black Bart Inn and Motel.** 55 St. Charles Street, San Andreas, CA 95249. With rooms available in both the historic inn and the adjacent motel, the Black Bart offers comfortable and inexpensive lodging. There's also a restaurant in the hotel, with a large salad bar, as well as a banquet room. $$. (209) 754–3808.

**Robin's Nest.** 247 St. Charles Street, San Andreas, CA 95249. For bed-and-breakfast accommodations, try this nineteenth-century Queen Anne. Nine rooms—five upstairs, four on the main floor—are decorated in period antiques. A well-known favorite of visitors to the area. $$–$$$. (209) 754–1076.

# ANGELS CAMP

Best known as the site of the annual Jumping Frog Jubilee in May, Angels Camp was founded by Henry Angel, who in 1848 opened a trading post to serve local gold seekers. The jumping-frog celebrations began in 1928, when civic boosters decided to use Mark Twain's first successful short story, "The Celebrated Jumping Frog of Calaveras County," as a way to draw tourists to the area. These days, the event, held the third weekend in May, draws thousands of contestants and their "trainers" from around the world. Not only is the town's nickname "Frogtown," but frogs are ubiquitous here, emblazoned on coffee cups and even stenciled onto city sidewalks. For information on entering the frog-jumping contest, call (209) 736–2561.

Angels Camp is located on CA-49 about 15 miles south of San Andreas.

## WHERE TO GO

**Calaveras County Visitors Center.** 1211 South Main (CA-49), Angels Camp, CA 95222-0637. Stop in here for brochures and other information on the wide range of activities in the area, from skiing at nearby Bear Valley to exploring the caverns that honeycomb much of the ground below the county's surface. Also, lots of current information on lodging, dining, shopping, and sight-seeing. (209) 736-0049.

## WHERE TO EAT

**The Pickle Barrel.** 1225 South Main, Angels Camp, CA 95222. A small deli-restaurant specializing in soups, pasta salads, and sandwiches as well as microbrews and local wines, the Pickle Barrel also serves full-course dinners, including prime rib and seafood. Open for lunch daily, dinner Friday and Saturday. $$-$$$. (209) 736-4704.

## WHERE TO STAY

**Angels Inn Motel.** 600 Main Street, Angels Camp, CA 95221. Centrally located, just north of downtown Angels Camp, this sixty-room recently remodeled motel has clean, nice-sized rooms (suites and kitchenettes available) and a large outdoor pool. $$. (209) 736-4242.

# Southeast Day Trip 2

Most folks traveling east on Highway 50 from Sacramento pass over Echo Summit, drop down into the Tahoe Basin, and continue on to Stateline, ignoring one of the prettiest routes and areas in the state. Instead of following the hordes of casino-bound motor homes, hang a right (south) turn in Myers, about 5 miles east of the "Y"—the junction of Highway 50 and CA-89 at South Shore—and take CA-89 south over Luther Pass (7,740 feet) to the much-less-traveled Markleeville-Carson Pass area. This region is characterized by rugged, fir- and pine-covered mountainsides, granite peaks pushing skyward well above timberline, and broad mountain meadows riven with meandering trout streams.

Not a whole lot to *do,* per se, on this trip, but if sight-seeing is what the doctor ordered, then this trip ought to fill the prescription.

## MARKLEEVILLE

Markleeville is a tiny mountain town on CA-89 about 12 miles south of the junction of CA-88 and CA-89. In former times a bustling lumber community, Markleeville is now better known for a handful of redneck bars and the nearby Grover Hot Springs (see below), a favorite escape for South Lake Tahoe residents.

The town was founded in 1861 by Jacob J. Marklee, who was killed in a land dispute the following year by another settler, Henry Tuttle, who claimed he had staked his claim to the same land before Marklee had. Tuttle was found innocent of the charges, the killing having been in self-defense. Markleeville was named seat of Alpine County in 1875. Until the bottom fell out of the silver market in the early 1890s, Markleeville was home to nearly 12,000 people; today fewer than one hundred people live here year-round.

## WHERE TO GO

**Alpine County Historical Complex.** 1 School Street, Box 517, Markleeville, CA 96120. This three-part complex includes a variety of historical displays designed to tell the story of Markleeville's rowdy past. **Old Webster School,** the town's original one-room school, built in 1882, has been completely restored, and its walls are decorated with artwork by former students. The **Old Log Jail,** which during the late nineteenth century provided lodging for Markleeville's ill-behaved, now houses gear and equipment from the area's mining, lumber, and farming heritage. The main **Museum** includes a blacksmithy, historical photos, nineteenth-century snow skis (used to help deliver mail), and Native American baskets and clothing.

The museum complex is open Thursday through Monday, Memorial Day through Labor Day. Small admission fee. (530) 694-2317.

**Grover Hot Springs.** A popular winter destination for South Lake Tahoe and Kirkwood skiers, Grover Hot Springs is a great place to soak away the day's aches after a day of winter-sports activities. Not bad the rest of the year, either: I've spent many a late afternoon in the warm waters, after a long day fishing the nearby streams. The springs are well marked, 4 miles northwest of Markleeville on Hot Springs Road. (530) 694-2248.

## "CA-88"

## BACK TO SACRAMENTO

Depending on the time of the year, and the weather, you can choose from a number of ways to get back to Sacramento from the Markleeville area. Of course, you can retrace your steps back through

Meyers on CA-89 and Highway 50, but keep in mind that traffic can be pretty bad going back over the pass. Sunday afternoons and evenings, especially, when weekenders are bailing out of the Tahoe Basin, traffic can be downright nasty.

You can also go back north on CA-89 as far as the junction with CA-88, at which point you can go west up over Carson Pass (8,573 feet) and then return to Sacramento via Jackson and Sutter Creek. A drive along CA-88 is practically a destination unto itself. This is an absolutely beautiful part of the state—broad meadows wet with snowmelt, towering peaks in the distance—and the road is much less traveled. Along the way you'll pass by Kirkwood Ski Area, one of California's premier ski resorts, with 2,300 acres of terrain and complete retail and rental facilities, as well as lodging and dining. During the off-season the resort offers mountain biking, hiking, and horseback riding. For information call (209) 258-6000.

You can also get back to Sacramento via CA-89, by continuing south from Markleeville to the CA-89/4 junction. Closed in winter over Ebbets Pass (8,730 feet), CA-4 drops down out of the high Sierra into the foothill gold rush country at Angels Camp (from Markleeville to Angels Camp is about 80 miles), where you can catch CA-49 north through San Andreas, Jackson, and Sutter Creek, then CA-16 west. From Angels Camp it's another 75 miles back to Sacramento.

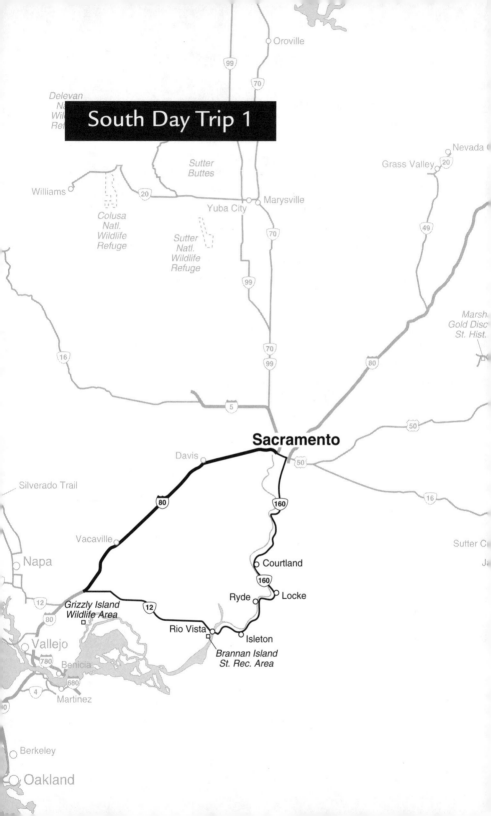

South Day Trip 1

Just minutes south of downtown Sacramento, the Sacramento River delta is one of those regions about which even many longtime Californians don't seem to know a whole lot. The state's major north-south artery, I–5, jogs around it to the east, while I–80, the main route between Sacramento and the Bay Area, steers well clear of its northern reaches. In other words, you don't happen upon the delta when you're headed elsewhere; you've got to plan to go.

This unique area supports a rich agricultural economy, and though many of the businesses long dependent on the once-thriving river-based trade are long gone—storefronts boarded up, gas stations rusted and ghostly—the area offers a fascinating look at an important part of the state. CA–160 and CA–12—from Sacramento to Rio Vista—wind along levees and over draw bridges from island to island, past former speakeasies dating from the 1920s, and provide views of sprawling orchards and the million-dollar homes of their owners. All the while the ever-widening Sacramento River, always in view, is dotted with giant yachts, tiny fishing boats, big boxy houseboats, and roaring speedboats pulling water-skiers in their rolling wakes.

The best way to get to the delta from Sacramento is to head south on CA–160. You'll be surprised how quickly the landscape changes dramatically. Just a few miles south of the sprawling tracts of suburban Sacramento, the road narrows, lifts up onto the levee tops, and soon becomes shoulderless, splitting pear orchards, with branches reaching nearly to the road.

Below is a small sampling of the many tiny hamlets that you'll find as you explore the delta region. Part of the fun of day-tripping through this area is simply following your intuitions. It's close enough to Sacramento that even if you find yourself following the road less taken and ending up on a levee with nothing but orchards or river sprawling before you, you can still turn around and be back in Sacramento in less than an hour and a half.

## COURTLAND

Courtland is a tiny pear-farming town on the east side of the river, most of the handful of buildings are safely below a 30-foot levee built up to keep the river in check at flood stage. Not much going on here unless you're a pear farmer, fisherman, or into stopping in for some surprisingly excellent grub.

### WHERE TO EAT

**Rosie's Rocking Docks.** 11740 Highway 160, Courtland, CA 95615. This is a classic little riverfront bar and restaurant, where fishermen, farmers, and Lycra-clad bicyclists rub elbows over fish and chips and ale and watch the river go by from the bar inside or the outside deck. Open for lunch daily and dinner on weekends, Rosie's specializes in steak sandwiches, burgers, and chicken-in-a-basket. Most Sunday afternoons there's live music outside on the deck in summer and inside the rest of the year. Even if you eat outside, be sure to go inside to check out the huge iguanas in terrariums. (*Smoke alert*: Rosie's doesn't seem to take much stock in California's ban on smoking in public places. I sat at the bar inside and was flanked by cigarette smokers, both of whom were offered ashtrays by Skip, Rosie's husband, who himself was sucking on a big stogie.) $$. (916) 775-1172.

**La Posada.** 11721 Highway 160, Courtland, CA 95615. This is one of the best little Mexican restaurants around, passing the Sacramento-Day-Trips Authenticity Test (see Guide to California Cuisine) with flying colors. The tamales alone being worth a trip well out of your way. Order them to eat in or to eat on the road, or, better yet, to stock up the freezer. They're $1.50 each. Other specials include carnitas, fajitas, and some twenty seafood dishes, including shrimp tostadas, fish tacos, and oysters on the half-shell. Open daily from 8:00 A.M. to 8:00 P.M. $–$$. (916) 775-1382.

## LOCKE

Even in an area full of towns that seem trapped in time, Locke, more than the others, is worth a visit. Known as the "last rural China-town," Locke was founded in the early twentieth century entirely by Chinese laborers and was once home to a population of more than 2,000 Chinese, who ran boardinghouses, markets, speakeasies, opium dens, and an opera. Present-day Locke, listed on the National Register of Historic Places, is a ghostly 1-block-long strip of wooden sidewalks and rickety structures still clearly manifesting their ancient Asian traditions and 100-year-old construction.

### WHERE TO EAT

**Al the Wop's.** 13943 Main Street, Locke, CA 95690. Dating from Locke's heyday and a linguistically less sensitive time, this sixty-five-year-old restaurant, despite its limited menu, is a favorite of folks from around the delta as well as of savvy passers-through. Try the chicken or New York steak, with a side of spaghetti, and try to ignore the stuffed moose heads eyeing your table. Open daily for lunch and dinner. $$. (916) 776-1800.

## RYDE

There was a time when the little town of Ryde was one of the most happenin' places in northern California. During Prohibition Ryde's main drag was the site of speakeasies and brothels, and if you knew the password, you could get into the Ryde Hotel's basement, a netherworld of flappers, gamblers, jazz, and gin. Pulling into Ryde today—after having crossed over the river from Locke and Walnut Grove—you can imagine bootleggers jamming down dusty levee roads, their trunks full of illegal booze, and arriving at back doors to make their deliveries to the strains of a Sydney Bechet–like soprano sax, or a Louis Armstrong trumpet, or even Al Jolsen himself, a regular.

## WHERE TO EAT AND STAY

**The Ryde Hotel,** 14340 Highway 160, Ryde, CA 95680. The Ryde presently operates as a restaurant and one of the few lodging options in the rural delta area. Completely renovated, but keeping with its Prohibition-era design, the hotel, a definite pink, stands out dramatically from its levee-top location, above the orchards sprawling behind it and the nine-hole golf course just to the south. The Ryde's dining room serves breakfast, lunch, and dinner on weekends, April through November, with a special Sunday brunch ($19.95). Lunches include crab cakes, burgers, sandwiches, and salads ($$), while the dinner menu offers steak, rack of lamb, duck, and salmon ($$$).

Rooms are available, with shared or private bath ($$), or you can get a suite with an in-room spa. ($$$). (916) 776–1318.

# ISLETON

Though much of Isleton's main drag now is boarded up, it, too, was at one time a bustling river town, with brothels and speakeasies attracting West Coast versions of Jay Gatsby and Tom Buchanan. Also, like many of the other towns in the delta, Isleton has a distinctly Chinese past, with Chinese laborers working the nearby fields and canneries, where, in the 1930s, some 90 percent of the country's asparagus was grown and processed.

## WHERE TO EAT AND STAY

**Rogelio's.** 34 Main Street, Isleton, CA 95641. Located in a remodeled early twentieth-century hotel, Rogelio's serves Chinese, Italian, and Mexican food for lunch and dinner. Offering burritos, shrimp chow mein, and veal scallopini all on the same menu, this is a local favorite, and folks swear it's all delicious. $$. Rogelio's also has ten remodeled hotel rooms available upstairs from the dining room, all with private baths. $$. (916) 777–5878.

## RIO VISTA

Highway 160 tees into Highway 12 just south of Isleton. Go left at this junction to Rio Vista, a small town on the west bank of the Sacramento River that dates back to the late 1850s, when it was called Los Brazos del Rio, or "Arms of the River." For such a small town, Rio Vista's got a surprising number of attractions, and the little community is definitely worth exploring for an afternoon.

### WHERE TO GO

**Rio Vista Chamber of Commerce.** 75 Main Street, Rio Vista, CA 94571. Lots of information on Rio Vista as well as the greater delta area, including literature on houseboating, waterskiing, fishing, and local attractions. For a visitor's packet call (707) 374-2700.

**Rio Vista Museum.** 16 North Front Street, Rio Vista, CA 94571. This storefront museum is much larger than it would appear from the outside, and the many rooms inside tell the story not only of Rio Vista but of much of the delta area. Learn more about Chinese contributions to the region, as well as about local agriculture, the huge underground natural-gas reservoir, and local veterans of overseas wars.

This is also an excellent place to find out what else there is to do in the area. Not only does museum literature designate things to see around Rio Vista, but the volunteer docents are fountains of information on exploring the delta area. Open weekend afternoons only. (707) 374-5169.

**Foster's Bighorn.** 143 Main Street, Rio Vista, CA 94571. Located just around the corner from the Rio Vista Museum, this bar and restaurant is home to the mounted heads of more than 300 animals from around the world, most of which were killed by big-game hunter William Foster, who opened the place in 1931. In addition to the expected deer, elk, moose, and bobcat, the walls at Foster's display lions, kudzu, a giraffe, hippopotamus, rhinoceros, Cape buffalo, walrus, and purportedly the largest (mounted) African elephant head on earth, the tusks and trunk of which hang out nearly halfway over the dining room. Regardless of your opinion of the ethics of trophy hunting, this place is worth checking out, if only for its sense of belonging to a very different time. Be sure to check out the photos on the walls, not only of Foster and other hunters with their kills and African guides but of natives in their natural environment and dress from the very early days of photography. Closed Mondays. (707) 374-2511.

**Humphrey the Whale Monument.** Foot of Main Street, Rio Vista, CA 94571. Humphrey was a wayward California gray whale that put Rio Vista on the map in 1985, when, apparently disoriented, he swam underneath the Golden Gate Bridge and somehow managed to find his way nearly 60 miles upriver to Rio Vista. For weeks the subject of an intense rescue effort by marine biologists, the navy, and local fishermen—who imitated killer-whale sounds (upriver), and gray-whale-mating sounds (downriver)—Humphrey finally headed back to sea to the cheers of Rio Vista locals. A monument to Humphrey is located in town where Main Street meets the water.

**Western Railway Museum.** Eleven miles west of Rio Vista on Highway 12. Offering 8-mile round-trip rides on an electric train, as well as displays of vintage rail- and streetcars, this museum, located midway between Rio Vista and Fairfield, is open weekends only. Small admission fee, with discounts for kids and seniors. Special seasonal events (Santa's onboard at Christmas) are also offered, and picnicking is available on the grounds. (707) 374-2978.

**Delta-area State Recreation Areas.** Two California State Recreation Areas in the delta region offer a range of outdoor opportunities, from picnicking and camping to fishing, boating, and windsurfing:

**Brannan Island Recreation Area.** Located on Highway 160 about 3 miles south of Rio Vista. Visitors expecting a recreation area akin to the gorgeously green ones in the Sierra Nevadas or along the coast might be disappointed, though the barren windswept spot offers its own stark beauty, if you look at it just right (what was that about the eye of the beholder?). Camping is available year-round, with reservations recommended spring through early fall. Facilities include RV sites, tent sites, and boat-in-only sites. Day users can take advantage of the public beach and picnic facilities. For information call (916) 777-6671, or write 17645 Highway 160, Rio Vista, CA 95471.

**Grizzly Island State Recreation Area.** This is farther west, with the turn off on Highway 12 about midway between Rio Vista and Fairfield. This is a popular area for birders—both hunters and watchers, depending on the season—because it's below the western flyway and attracts millions of waterfoul to its marshes. You can also view tule elk, a species thought to be extinct in the mid-nineteenth century but which have thrived here and in other places in the West, where they've been reintroduced and protected. For information call (707) 425-3828.

## WHERE TO EAT

**Foster's Bighorn.** 143 Main Street, Rio Vista, CA 94571. If you don't mind being eyed by some 300 dead animals, not to mention the mounted birds and fish, you can get good food at Foster's. Entrees include veal, lamb, prime rib, and seafood. $$-$$$. (707) 374-2511.

    **Jessen's Bar and Restaurant.** 95 Main Street, Rio Vista, CA 94571. This is another local favorite, at the foot of Main Street, almost on the water. In addition to the fried chicken and dumplings, the house specialty, you can also get steaks, seafood, and salads, as well as burgers and other sandwiches. Open Monday through Wednesday for lunch, Thursday through Sunday for lunch and dinner. $$-$$. (707) 374-6004.

## WHERE TO STAY

Not much in the way of lodging down this way, though in nearby Antioch or Fairfield, plenty of hotels and motels are available. In Rio Vista the **Rio Sands Lodge,** 205 Highway 12, Rio Vista, CA 94571, has clean, decent-sized rooms. $-$$. (707) 374-6374.

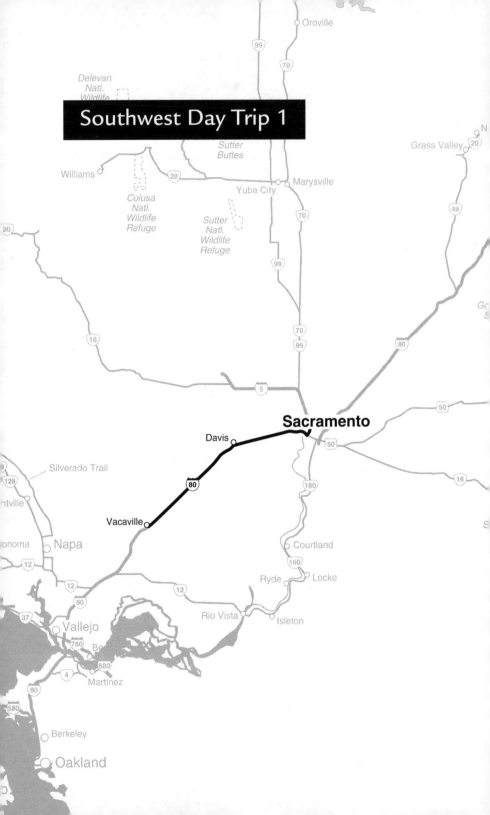

Southwest Day Trip 1

SOUTHWEST DAY TRIP 1

Davis
Vacaville

This short excursion from Sacramento offers a mind-boggling study in contrasts. Visit the quiet, rural university town of Davis, best known as a haunt of serious students of agriculture, animal husbandry, engineering, and etiology (grape growing and wine making), and then head on down the road to Vacaville, the site of one of the largest factory-stores malls in the country, where shoppers rush from store to store, their arms loaded with bargains.

## DAVIS

Located 15 miles west of Sacramento on I–80, downtown Davis is the city's center for culture, business, and entertainment. The large downtown area, spanning more than 60 blocks, is home to a myriad of entertainment venues, retail businesses, art galleries, bookstores, coffee shops, restaurants, and hotels.

### WHERE TO GO

**Davis Chamber of Commerce.** 228 B Street, Davis, CA 95616. Visitor information is available here not only on the town and surrounding area but on the attractions and events at the nationally acclaimed University of California at Davis (see below). (530) 756–5160.

    **University of California at Davis (UCD).** Located adjacent to downtown Davis, the university offers many special events throughout the academic year. Picnic Day, the campus's open house, occurs in April. This student-run event includes a parade, student exhibits, department exhibits, and food vendors. Animal attractions such as the Frisbee catching competition and the dachshund races are local favorites. Picnic Day also includes the Battle of the Bands, an explosive music battle, between different marching bands. Another UCD special event is the Whole Earth Festival, which takes place on Mother's Day weekend in May. Attending this weekend-long festival is like traveling back to the sixties. Women and men adorned with flowers, braids, bell-bottoms, and tie-dyed clothing are in abundance. The festival's goal is to promote holistic living; as such, recycling and compost bins are positioned throughout the festival. A variety of speakers, dancers, poets, and bands perform on the two main stages, while other forms of entertainment surround festival goers. More than one hundred booths containing hand-crafted goods, environmental information, interactive games, and an array of multicultural foods guarantee a good time is had by all. A great place for free entertainment, tasting new foods, watching people, and enjoying the earth. (530) 752–1011.

**Davis Musical Theater Company.** Performances located at the Varsity Theater. 616 Second Street, Davis, CA 95616. Founded in 1984 by Jan and Steve Isaacson, this local theater company offers musical performances year-round. The Theater Company, which is an all-volunteer organization, provides high-quality, family entertainment at reasonable prices. The company brings six Broadway musicals to Davis each season. Call the box office for current production information, tickets, and reservations. (530) 756–3682.

**Explorit!** 3141 Fifth Street, Davis, CA 95616. Founded in 1982, this interactive museum specializes in science, math, and technology. Designed to arouse curiosity while entertaining, the science center's goal is to promote learning in a fun atmosphere. Through lectures, exhibitions, and special events, the science center allows people of all ages to experience and learn how science affects everyday life. Themes change every eight weeks. (530) 756–0191.

**The Farmer's Market.** Located in Central Park, Fourth Street and C Street, Davis, CA . Local farmers, merchants, and craftspeople display and sell their goods. Vendors sell fresh fruit, vegetables, and baked goods; pottery, artwork, and other handcrafted goods; and house and outdoor plants. Live entertainment is often provided. The market is held on Wednesday afternoons and Saturday mornings, weather permitting. From May through September the Wednesday hours are extended for Picnic in the Park market, a summer market that contains more booths, free entertainment, and activities for the whole family. Call ahead to confirm dates and for times. (530) 756-1695.

**The Palms Playhouse.** 726 Drummond Avenue, Davis, CA 95616. Located in South Davis, The Palms Playhouse is an eclectic and intimate concert venue. The Palms brings a sizzling mix of jazz, blues, folk, bluegrass, and more to this college town. Palms favorites include Roy Rogers, Norton Buffalo, Little Charlie & the Nightcats, and Chris Webster of Mumbo Gumbo fame. While no seat in this intimate setting is bad, seating is on a first-come-first-serve basis, so large groups should arrive early to assure sitting together. The wooden folding chairs are hard, so bring a pillow for cushioning. For information about the current schedule, call (530) 756-9901. Armadillo Music offers tickets without a surcharge. (530) 758-8058.

**The Pottery Place.** 132 E Street, Lower Level, Mansion Square, Davis, CA 95616. This "paint it yourself" pottery studio allows everyone to express her creative side. A wide selection of pottery pieces is ready to be painted, fired, and made into an original piece of artwork. All glazes are nontoxic and are food, microwave, and dishwasher safe, making your artwork fun and functional. Drop-ins are welcome, and reservations can be made for birthday parties, wedding showers, and other special occasions. Gift certificates are also available. (530) 750-2165.

**Arboretum.** Located on the UCD campus, this scenic arboretum is home to more than 4,000 kinds of trees and plants. With paved paths running alongside both banks of Putah Creek, the arboretum is perfect for walkers, joggers, skaters, and bicyclists. While walking along the banks of the creek, it is not uncommon to come across students napping on the grass, children of all ages feeding the ducks, and blissful couples saying their wedding vows. The spacious grass areas make the arboretum a perfect setting for a game of catch or for throwing a Frisbee. The arboretum also provides a beautiful surrounding for a picnic or a relaxing day away from the sounds of the city.

**Campus Cinema.** Chem 194, located on the UCD campus, is a chemistry lecture hall by day and a student-run movie theater during selected weekends. Campus Cinema offers both Dolby Digital and DTS sound systems. Campus Cinema offers sneak previews of unreleased movies and also shows previously released films. Campus Cinema also holds a film festival each year called The UCD Independent/International Film Festival. Prices are lower than standard movie theater prices. Call the film hotline for movie listings. (530) 752-FILM.

**UC Davis Athletics.** See the UC Davis Aggies in action! With the exciting victory of the men's basketball team at the 1998 NCAA Division II Tournament has come an increased interest in Aggie sports. In addition to basketball, UC Davis offers a diverse selection of competitive sports such as football, swimming, diving, gymnastics, wrestling, and track and field. UC Davis sponsors twenty-three sports, so there is always a sporting event scheduled. Call the Campus Box Office for dates, times, and prices at (530) 752-1915 or the Aggie Sports Hotline at (530) 752-1700.

### WHERE TO SHOP

**The Artery.** 207 G Street, Davis, CA 95616. The Artery is both a store and gallery featuring original artwork from more than forty northern California artists. The Artery features jewelry, ceramics, paintings, photographs, sculptures, and more, and offers gift certificates, gift wrapping, bridal registry, and layaway plans. (530) 758-8330.

**Bogey's Books.** 223 E Street, Davis, CA 95616. This centrally located bookstore has an assortment of new, used, and out-of-print books. Bogey's has a diverse selection of books including fiction, nonfiction, science fiction, mystery, children's, cooking, politics, and art. If a book is not in stock, it usually can be ordered. The atmosphere is comfortable, and the staff is friendly and helpful. With lounge chairs placed throughout the store, Bogey's is the perfect place to sit back, relax, and read. (530) 757-6127.

### WHERE TO EAT

**Caffe Italia.** 1121 Richards Boulevard, Davis, CA 95616. Specializing in Italian dishes, Caffe Italia offers a selection of soups, salads, sandwiches, pizzas, and pasta dishes. The food is delicious, the service is prompt, and the staff is friendly. Everything on the menu can be ordered to go, and the Caffe also offers catering. $$. (530) 758-7200.

**The Crepe Bistro.** 234 E Street, Davis, CA 95616. This restaurant is one of Davis' hidden treasures, featuring a variety of mouthwatering French and Cajun dishes. This small, friendly, dimly lit bistro brings a touch of Paris to Davis through its decor and fabulous crepes. Inside, you get an instant sensation of the coziness that makes a good locale, so place an order at the counter, grab a table, and wait for the delicious food to arrive. $-$$. (530) 753-2575.

**Mishka's Cafe.** 514 Second Street, Davis, CA 95616. A local study hangout for UC Davis students, as well as a great place to enjoy an espresso, coffee, or cup of tea. Coffee beans are roasted in the center of the cafe, visible to customers. Mishka's also offers a selection of pastries, salads, soups, sandwiches, and ice cream. On selected evenings Mishka's Cafe provides live entertainment; for current schedule call (530) 753-8639. $-$$. For information regarding cafe hours call (530) 759-0811.

**Soga's Restaurant & Bar.** 217 E Street, Davis, CA 95616. Specializing in California cuisine, this gourmet restaurant offers homemade soups, fresh fish, vegetarian entrees, meat entrees, and pasta in an elegant setting. Soga's also offers an extensive selection of wines and a full bar. Intimate seating is available, making Soga's perfect for a romantic evening. Large banquet parties can also be accommodated. Indoor as well as patio seating is available. Reservations should be made for weekend dining. $$$. (530) 757-1733.

**Sophia's Thai Kitchen.** 129 E Street, Orange Court Building E, Davis, CA 95616. Owned and operated by Guido and Sophia Patterson, Sophia's Thai Kitchen is one of Davis's hidden treats. Sophia's offers a wide selection of authentic Thai food made with the freshest ingredients and served in a pleasant atmosphere. Both vegetarian and meat dishes are available and can be ordered either mild or hot and spicy. Sophia's offers both indoor and outdoor seating, as well as traditional Thai seating in the Thai Room. $$. (530) 758-4333.

## WHERE TO STAY

**Aggie Inn.** 245 First Street, Davis, CA 95616. Located 1 block from UC Davis and near central Davis, the Aggie Inn offers more than an excellent location. Each suite includes a refrigerator, a microwave, and a coffeemaker. Among the amenities offered are a sauna, a spa, and a complimentary continental breakfast. The inn also offers a conference facility, which can be reserved for private use. UC Davis campus maps are available at the front desk. $$. (530) 756-0352.

**Best Western Palm Court Hotel.** 234 D Street, Davis, CA 95616. This luxurious hotel is located in the heart of Davis. There are twenty-seven suites, each furnished with ornate artwork and antiques. Each suite includes a refrigerator, a mini wet bar, a hair dryer, a telecall, a television, an ironing board, and an iron. The hotel offers an Executive Boardroom, which can be reserved for private functions. On-site there is also an exercise facility, a sauna, and a spa. Overnighters are offered a complimentary continental breakfast provided in the exquisite atrium. Adjacent to the hotel are Cafe Bernardo and Bar Bernardo. $$$. (530) 753-7100.

**Hallmark Inn.** 110 F Street, Davis, CA 95616. Located 5 blocks from UC Davis, in downtown Davis, this inn offers overnighters a complimentary breakfast, as well as complimentary cocktails, wine, beer, and soft drinks. The inn also offers full use of the Davis Racquet and Fitness Center (off-site) and a large pool (on-site). The inn also has two conference rooms available for private use. Adjacent to the inn is a twenty-four-hour restaurant. $$. (530) 753-3600.

**University Inn Bed & Breakfast.** 340 A Street, Davis, CA 95616. With just four rooms, this bed-and-breakfast offers a charming setting. Furnished with country decor and situated across from UC Davis, the inn offers visitors a generous breakfast, complimentary fresh fruit, coffee, tea, and flowers, as well as bicycles to borrow. $$. (530) 756-8648.

# VACAVILLE

About 18 miles west of Davis on the well-traveled I-80, Vacaville is a sprawling community that in the past decade has lost sight of much of its individuality—not to mention its history as an important ranching and farming center—as a monstrous factory-stores mall, mega-warehouse stores, fast-food franchises, and *lots* of pavement have swallowed a huge portion of the town's outlying areas.

Though Vacaville translates into Spanish as "cowtown," it was actually named for Don Manuel Vaca, one of the area's original ranchers. When I was a kid in the 1960s and traveling with my parents in the old Plymouth wagon, my brothers and I could always tell when we were near Vacaville, even if we had our eyes closed: The town smelled of onions, *all the time* (or so it seemed). Onions are no longer processed in Vacaville, and about the only whiff of them you're likely to get is from the In-and-Out Burger or perhaps the Fresh Choice restaurant, both right along the highway. Additionally, Vacaville was at one time home to the famous Nut Tree Restaurant, a venerable roadside eatery that served generations of travelers for most of the twentieth century. Alas, the Nut Tree closed down in the mid-1990s, and today the sprawling fields due west are the site of the annual Renaissance Pleasure Faire, a Bay Area tradition (late August through early October) that moved to Vacaville in 1999 after some thirty years in Novato.

This is also the site of the California Medical Facility at Vacaville, which has housed numerous famous prisoners over the years, from Black Panther members to Charlie Manson, who every once in a while still comes up for parole, which, of course, is invariably denied.

## WHERE TO GO

**The Factory Stores.** Well, so this isn't the most insightful advice you've ever read in a travel guide. You gotta do it, gotta visit the factory stores. Even if you're not a shopper. Take a cruise through the parking lots. You'll be amazed at the sheer size of the mall and the number of stores, as well as the way consumerism seems to have become nearly a religion—all bow down at the temple of the Nike discount store.

To be fair, there truly are reasons to shop here. Sometimes you can find closeouts and seconds for a fraction of what you would pay in a regular retail store. But be forewarned: It's easy to get caught up in the frenzy and to forget that not all the deals are that great. I've found that Levis, for example, on sale at Mervyn's are often less expensive than at the Levis factory outlet.

Other stores include London Fog, Nike, Mikasa, Adidas, Bass Shoes, Carter's Children's Clothes, Bugle Boy, Samsonite, and of course specialty stores with kitchenware, socks, leather goods, sweaters, books, and sporting goods. My own personal favorites, and I realize I'm exposing my biases here, include Black and Decker and Big Dogs.

**Vacaville Museum.** 213 Buck Avenue, Vacaville, CA 95687. If the culture of the factory stores isn't exactly your cup of tea, check out this little museum that celebrates the history and natural history of Vacaville and Solano County. In addition to historical photos and other artifacts, the museum displays native flora, and docents offer guided tours of historic downtown Vacaville. Open Wednesday through Sunday; donations accepted. (707) 447-4513.

## WHERE TO EAT

A plethora of restaurants has sprouted up to feed shoppers, famished and exhausted after a day of signing credit-card receipts. Plenty of fast-food outlets, including **In-and-Out Burger** and **McDonald's,** but there are also some pretty decent places to sit down and enjoy a good meal.

**Fresh Choice.** 1001 Helen Power Drive, Vacaville, CA 95687. I love this place. Inexpensive, convenient, healthful. I wouldn't make the place a destination, but it's perfect for lunch or dinner when you're on the road. Basically, it's a classic all-you-can-eat buffet with an emphasis on healthful food. Lots of different kinds of salads (from Caesar to Thai chicken), as well as a huge assortment of vegetables and other salad makings to create your own. There are also excellent homemade soups, pastas, and fresh breads. Open for lunch and dinner daily. $$. (707) 446-1056.

**Black Oak Restaurant.** 320 Orange Drive, Vacaville, CA 95687. This classic roadside coffeehouse and restaurant has been around for decades, having once been an alternative to the Nut Tree across the highway. Thankfully, it has survived the growth nearby and remains a quiet little oasis amid the craziness. Standard roadhouse fare, from salads and burgers to soup and chicken-fried steaks. Open for breakfast, lunch, and dinner daily. $-$$. (707) 448-1311.

**Chevy's.** 200 Nut Tree Parkway, Vacaville, CA 95688. This chain of Mexican restaurants uses only fresh ingredients in all its dishes and has been very successful in establishing itself throughout California. The food is very good, and the atmosphere is festive.

Designate a driver and order one of their *grande* margaritas. $$.
(707) 469–0280.

## WHERE TO STAY

**Best Western Heritage Inn.** 1420 East Monte Vista, Vacaville, CA
95688. Located on the frontage road near shopping and restaurants,
this relatively new lodge offers clean, good-sized rooms at reasonable
rates. $$. (707) 448–8453.

**Courtyard By Marriott.** 120 Nut Tree Parkway, Vacaville, CA
95688. This is the area's newest and largest hotel/motel (130 rooms).
Some suites available, some rooms with whirlpools. $$. (707)
451–9000.

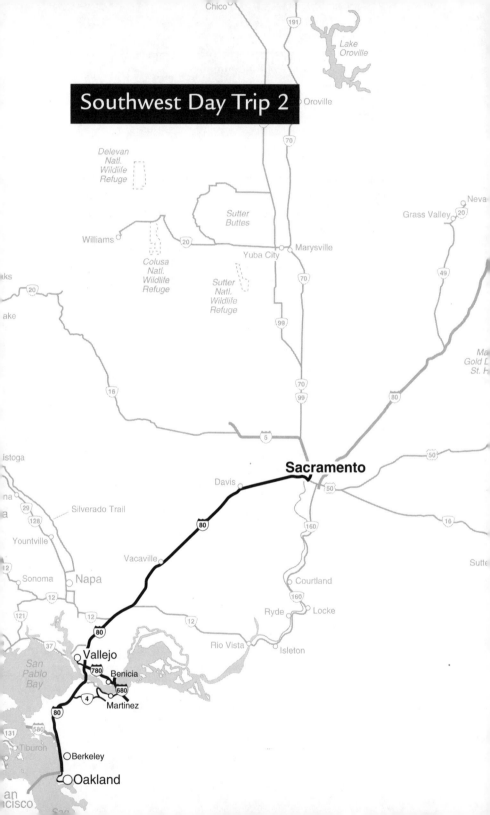

SOUTHWEST DAY TRIP 2

Vallejo
Benicia · Martinez
Berkeley · Oakland

Barring traffic jams, you can be in what locals call the East Bay in less than an hour and a half after leaving Sacramento. On the other hand, if you get caught in commute traffic, especially if there's been an accident that slows things down even more—quite common in this area, one of the most densely populated areas in the state—you could spend just about that same hour and a half stopping and going and eventually traveling not much farther than you could have walked in the same amount of time.

This means, of course, that though a day trip from Sacramento to Berkeley and Oakland is feasible, timing is everything. Don't plan on being on one of the major commute arteries—I-80, I-580, and I-880, especially—on weekdays between, say 7:00 and 9:00 A.M. or between 3:00 and 6:00 P.M.

Weekends it's not so bad. You could head out of Sacramento at 8:00 on a Saturday morning and be in Berkeley by around 9:30, spend the day exploring the area, get back in your car at 4:00 P.M. and be home by 5:30.

It's a straight shot from Sacramento to the East Bay, I-80 taking you mostly uninterestingly from the valley's center to the hills of the Bay Area and the cooler, salty air.

## VALLEJO

Once you hit Vallejo, you're in the Bay Area proper, although technically this city is actually on the shore of San Pablo Bay, a northern arm of San Francisco Bay. Founded in 1851 by General Mariano Vallejo, where the Napa River flows into the bay, the town served twice in the nineteenth century as the state capital. Today, Vallejo is a sprawling, mostly blue-collar city of more than 110,000 people. Recently, Vallejo has seen a large influx of transplants from San Francisco and the East Bay who've moved here because of its affordability. A recent *San Francisco Chronicle* article pointed out Vallejo's growing, and increasingly active, gay community, who have transformed many of Vallejo's historic neighborhoods by remodeling and painting old homes. One neighborhood, St. Vincent Hill, has taken on the moniker Lavender Hill after the colors of the gay-pride movement, and in November of 1999, an openly gay Vallejo attorney was elected to the city council.

Vallejo is also home to the California Maritime Academy, as well as dozens of mothballed U.S. Navy ships that sit in harbor at the Mare Island Naval Shipyard at the mouth of the Napa River.

The Vallejo Ferry connects San Francisco and Vallejo with regular service. From the Vallejo waterfront you can take a shuttle to Marine World/Africa USA or to the wine country.

## WHERE TO GO

**Marine World/Africa USA.** Marine World Parkway, Vallejo, CA 94589. This 160-acre theme park offers everything from killer-whale shows to roller-coaster rides. Visitors can enjoy the Shark Experience, the Elephant Encounter, and other wildlife exhibits, and from what I understand, you can also pay good money to buckle yourself into a tiny little cart, attached to a twisting pair of rails, and get upside and sideways, high above the sanity of *tierra firma*. There's also a petting zoo, a butterfly exhibit, and seasonal water-ski shows. *Caution:* Last I heard, lines for the rides were said to be exceptionally long; one visitor described it as a "madhouse." Plus, the roller coasters themselves have dramatically uglified the place. The skyline, once defined by the gentle greens of eucalyptus trees, is now dominated by brightly painted roller-coaster rails contorting into the air high above the tree limbs. Open daily. Admission about $25 for adults, $20 for kids; elephant rides and parking extra. (707) 643-6722.

**Vallejo Chamber of Commerce.** 2 Florida Street, Vallejo, CA 94590. Here you can get information on lodging, dining, and other attractions, as well as ferry and shuttle schedules. (707) 644-5551.

## WHERE TO STAY

**Holiday Inn Marine World/Africa USA.** 1000 Fairgrounds Drive, Vallejo, CA 94589. Adjacent to Marine World (save money on parking), this new hotel caters to theme-park visitors but also offers convenience for passers-through. Located near the junction of I-80 and CA-37 (connecting to the north Bay Area). Restaurant on the premises. $$-$$$. (707) 644-1200.

# BENICIA

Just a few miles west of Vallejo on I-80, take I-780 south to Benicia, a tiny town at the mouth of the Sacramento River. Like Vallejo, Benicia was also a one-time California state capital (1853-4). The historic downtown area, where the old capitol building still stands, is worth a side trip, particularly since the area has recently experienced a rejuvenation, with coffee shops, restaurants, galleries, and specialty shops moving into century-and-a-half-old buildings.

## WHERE TO GO

**Benicia Chamber of Commerce.** 610 First Street, Benicia, CA 94510. Stop in here to pick up maps for walking tours of historic Benicia, as well as more information on dining, lodging, and recreation in the area. (707) 745-2120.

**Benicia State Capitol Historic Park.** First and G Streets, Benicia, CA 94510. Celebrating the thirteen months that Benicia was the state's third capital, this restored building formerly housed the assembly, senate, and treasury. Small admission fee. (707) 745-3385.

## WHERE TO EAT

**Union Hotel.** 401 First Street, Benicia, CA 94510. A longtime local favorite, this restaurant serves upscale California cuisine in an elegant 1880s-vintage building. The menu varies, but you can count on local ingredients and healthful entrees—salads, seafood, pastas. Closed Mondays. $$-$$$. (707) 746-0100.

## MARTINEZ

Across the river from Benicia, Martinez was founded in the 1870s by Italian immigrants, whose favorite, and most famous, son is the great Joe DiMaggio. Local boosters claim it was also where the martini was invented, though other locales have also claimed the gin-and-vermouth classic as their own.

### WHERE TO GO

**John Muir National Historic Site.** 4202 Alhambra Avenue, Martinez, CA 94553. This is the last home of naturalist, orchardist, inventor, explorer, conservationist, author, and editor John Muir, who lived here the last twenty-four years of his life. Muir also co-founded the Sierra Club and was instrumental in the creation of the United States Forest Service, as well as in establishing five national parks. Muir's seventeen-room home, built in 1882, is open to the public; you can also tour the surrounding grounds. The home is decorated with original furnishings. Open Wednesday through Sunday; small admission fee. (510) 228-8860.

## BERKELEY

There are a number of ways to get to Berkeley from Martinez. You can continue south on I-780, through Concord, and then take I-680/CA-24 west to I-880 and go north. You can take CA-4 north from Martinez back to I-80 and continue west. Or you can take the scenic back roads, past Briones Regional Park and Briones Reservoir. To get to downtown Berkeley from I-80, take the University Avenue exit and go east. University Avenue dead-ends into the campus.

Berkeley is one of those cities whose reputation precedes it. A wonderful and eccentric blend of leftist intellectualism, counterculture ideologies, and artistic experimentation, Berkeley has been alternately nicknamed "The People's Republic of Berkeley" and "Ten

Square Miles Surrounded By Reality," not to mention the classic "Berserkley."

Berkeley was the focus of the famous Free Speech Movement of the 1960s, and it's where the Symbionese Liberation Army kidnapped newspaper heiress Patricia Hearst in 1974. These days things are a lot calmer. Though it's still a bastion of progressive politics, as well as one of the last hippie holdouts, the strident student protests of the past have been mostly replaced by study groups, poetry readings (and slams!), and folks enjoying good conversation over a latte or an expensive glass of Napa Valley merlot with an entree from a restaurant world-famous for its California cuisine. At the same time SUVs and Volvo wagons have all but replaced the once-requisite Volkswagen vans.

At any rate it's got to be at the top of any list of places to see in California, from the world-class university to Telegraph Avenue, where you can still buy tie-dyed T-shirts and hemp jewelry from street vendors. One could easily spend weeks here, getting to know the quirky community, the scores of tiny international restaurants, and the wonderful used-book stores.

## WHERE TO GO

**Berkeley Convention and Visitors Bureau.** 2015 Center Street, Berkeley, CA 94704. This is a good place to get oriented. Pick up maps of the area, including designated walking tours and recreation areas. There's also lots of information on dining, lodging, transportation, and other attractions in the area. Open weekdays only. (510) 549-7040.

**University of California at Berkeley.** Start at the **Visitor Information Center** (2200 University Avenue), where you can either pick up a map or take a guided tour of the campus. Among the places you'll want to visit are **Sproul Plaza** (where in 1964 Mario Savo laid the foundations of the Free Speech Movement), **Bancroft Library, Museum of Anthropology, University Art Museum,** and the outdoor **Greek Theater.** For information on tour schedules, call (510) 642-5215.

**Telegraph Avenue.** No visit to Berkeley is complete without a stroll down Telegraph Avenue. Here you can buy just about anything and everything you can imagine, from street vendors or from quirky retail shops. Looking for a tie-dyed T-shirt with a picture of Bob Marley on it? Look no further. Looking for that album (yes, album! *not* CD) by Moby Grape? Look no further. Looking for ways to expand your, well, way of viewing the world? Look no further . . .

**Charles Lee Tilden Regional Park.** This large city park (usually called simply Tilden Park) offers everything from swimming and golfing to train rides, a botanic garden, and hiking, biking, and equestrian trails, as well as an Environmental Education Center. Entrance to the park is free; small fees for train and pony rides and merry-go-round. (510) 562-7272.

**Bookstores.** One could easily spend an afternoon—or a weekend, for that matter—just exploring Berkeley's bookstores. The used-book stores, especially, provide excellent opportunities to browse, whether you're looking for specific titles and authors or prefer to wander without direction, letting one idea suggest another. The two best bookstores in town are the four-story **Moe's,** 2476

Telegraph Avenue (510-849-2087) and the giant **Cody's,** 2454 Telegraph Avenue (510-845-7852).

## WHERE TO EAT

Part of the fun of a visit to Berkeley is exploring new places to eat. Menus are often posted on doors or front windows so that you can get a sense of food prices before going inside and sitting down. And of course, like everything else in Berkeley, there's an impressively wide diversity of restaurants: tiny three-table burrito shops and pizzerias catering to student budgets, brew pubs, a wide variety of Asian restaurants, and upscale dining establishments famous around the country. Berkeley has become such an epicenter of dining that one section of town—rippling outward from Shattuck around Rose, Virginia, and Vine—has become known as the Gourmet Ghetto.

**Peet's Coffee.** 2124 Vine Street, Berkeley, CA 94709. Serving the very best coffee in the state (Peet's also supplies roasted beans to coffee shops around the West), this is a coffee connoisseur's heaven. Try the house blend, or a cup of French roast, or the Hawaiian, African, and South American specials. Excellent pastries to go with; (510) 841-0564. There are other Peet's locations throughout the Bay Area, including two more in Berkeley, at 2916 Domingo (510-843-1434), and at 1825 Solano (510-526-9607).

**Venezia.** 1799 University Avenue, Berkeley, CA 94709. For reasonably priced Italian food and a low-key atmosphere, you can't do much better than this local favorite. Highlights include homemade pastas, as well as free soup and salad with your meal. For appetizers try the "plate o' clams." Open daily for dinner, weekdays for lunch. $$. (510) 849-4681.

**Cha-Am.** 1543 Shattuck Avenue, Berkeley, CA 94709. One of the first Thai restaurants in the area, Cha-Am, according to my gourmand friend, Berkeleyite Alix Schwartz, has the best Thai food in town and is "everybody's favorite." Very reasonably priced and with a glassed-in patio providing open, airy seating. Open daily for lunch and dinner. $$. (510) 848-9664.

**Picante Cocina.** 1328 Sixth Street, Berkeley, CA 94710. In an area chock-full of excellent Mexican restaurants, this is one of the best, authentic, and at the same time innovative. Among the specialties are tamales, chile rellenos, and homemade tortillas. Open for lunch (Sunday brunch) and dinner daily. $-$$. (510) 525-3121.

**Rivoli.** 1539 Solano Avenue, Berkeley, CA 94707. A favorite of locals looking for a bit of a splurge, Rivoli features inventive California cuisine with a southern-European twist. Look for feta-cheese salad dressings, lots of garlic and rosemary, and lamb and seafood dishes. Be sure to check out the garden area, where roly-poly, well-fed raccoons stop by nightly to raid the cat-food bowls. Open for dinner daily. $$-$$$. (510) 526-2542.

**Chez Panisse.** 1517 Shattuck Avenue, Berkeley, CA 94709. This restaurant is almost solely responsible for the huge boom in California cuisine, and owner-chef Alice Waters is synonymous with all that's good about the trend. Using natural ingredients—wholly organic when possible—this little restaurant features a fixed-price menu that changes regularly, depending on the season and what produce is available. Count on fresh breads, creative appetizers, soups, and salads, and entrees often decked out in herbs, fruit, and unexpected greens. Closed Sundays. $$$. (510) 548-5525. Upstairs is a less expensive cafe, specializing in pastas, wood-fired pizzas, and grilled fish. $$. (510) 548-5049.

## WHERE TO STAY

**Bancroft Hotel.** 2680 Bancroft Way, Berkeley, CA 94704. This small (twenty-two rooms), "luxury boutique" hotel offers convenience and relatively inexpensive lodging directly across the street from the UC campus. Rates include breakfast. $$-$$$. (510) 549-1000.

**Berkeley City Club.** 2315 Durant Avenue, Berkeley, CA 94704. A thirty room converted home designed by Julia Morgan, this inn also offers easy access to the campus and is frequently used by out-of-town lecturers and other UC guests. $$$. (510) 848-7800.

**Berkeley Marina Radisson Hotel.** 200 Marina Boulevard, Berkeley, CA 94710. Just off I-80 on the west side, this 375-room motel/hotel offers easy access to downtown Berkeley (it's just off University Avenue), without the hassles of traffic and parking. Clean, safe, and good-sized rooms. $$$. (510) 548-7920.

**Holiday Inn Express Hotel and Suites.** 1175 University Avenue, Berkeley, CA 94702. Berkeley's newest accommodations (March

2000), this hotel offers seventy-plus rooms and easy access to campus and the rest of the Bay Area. $$$. (510) 548-1700.

## OAKLAND

Oakland is directly adjacent to Berkeley on the south side. Driving from one city to the next, you probably won't realize when you've crossed over. To get to downtown Oakland from Berkeley, continue south on I-80/880, staying on 880, when 80 doglegs west (right) toward the Bay Bridge and San Francisco.

Like Berkeley, Oakland has a reputation that often precedes it. Unfortunately, it has never really been a favorable one, and the reputation isn't really very accurate or fair. Granted, the gap between the haves and have-nots here is—as many people point out—painfully wide. Plus, the city's public schools are in terrible shape—prompting a good friend of mine to pack up the family and move to Flagstaff, Arizona, when his oldest son was four. And as if that weren't bad enough, Oakland's overpasses and buildings were destroyed in the Loma Prieta earthquake of 1989, and in the mid-1990s, scores of the city's most expensive homes were lost in a gigantic fire that burned out of control for days in the Oakland hills.

Yet things have been changing, thanks in large part to the current mayor, former California governor Jerry Brown, who has managed to help rejuvenate the economy and inject a sense of civic pride into the city's populace. Overpasses have been rebuilt—most of the city roadways and buildings been retrofitted to make them less prone to earthquake damage—and new homes have replaced those torched by the Oakland-hills fire.

And even though the best-known quote about Oakland is native-daughter Gertrude Stein's quip, "There is no there there," others have been kinder. Contemporary novelist Terry McMillan, who lived in Oakland when she was a college student, said it's "one of the most culturally alive cities I've come to know," and native Oaklander singer Shiela E. says, "Oakland will always be a big part of my life."

## WHERE TO GO

**Oakland Visitors Center.** Jack London Square, Broadway and Embarcadero, Oakland, CA 94607. Whether you're here for the afternoon or are moving out from Kansas, this is a good first stop. In addition to everything you'd expect in terms of information on lodging, dining, and transportation, pick up literature on Oakland's myriad historical, cultural, and commercial attractions, far too numerous to specify here. You can also get maps to historical walking tours. For guided tours call the **Oakland Tours Program** at (510) 238–3234.

**Oakland Museum of California.** 1000 Oak Street, Oakland, CA 94607. This large, three-part museum complex covers just about everything and anything that reflects California history, culture, and natural environment, with an emphasis on the state's diversity in every arena. From the state's Native American days through the Spanish movement on through the gold rush and the early days of

Bay Area blues and Beat poetry, from wildlife to sports to painting and sculpture—if it's part of what makes California California, you'll find it here. Open Wednesday through Sunday; $5.00 admission. (510) 238–2200.

**African-American Museum and Library.** 659 Fourteenth Street, Oakland, CA 94612. This museum and resource center emphasizes the contributions and experiences of Oakland's and the East Bay's African-American population. Call for hours. (510) 238–4974.

**Oakland Asian Cultural Center.** 388 Ninth Street, Oakland, CA 94607. Offering art exhibits, educational workshops, and meeting facilities, this colorful cultural center "seeks to foster cross-cultural understanding" among non-Asian, traditional Asian, and modern Asian-American people. It's the largest Asian-American cultural center in the country. (510) 208–6080.

**Lake Merritt.** California's first wildlife refuge (1870), Lake Merritt and the surrounding 122-acre Lakeside Park combine to provide an environment unique to a city the size of Oakland's, which completely encompasses this natural saltwater lake. Among the many diversions and attractions the park offers are **Children's Fairyland,** a ten-acre theme park for kids ten and under, at Grand and Bellevue Avenues (510–238–6876); the **Sailboat House,** where you can rent paddleboats, rowboats, and windsurfers, 568 Bellevue Avenue (510–444–3807); and the **Camron-Stratford House,** an elegant, open-to-the-public restored Victorian, 1418 Lakeside (510–836–1976). To get to Bellevue Avenue, take Broadway north from downtown and turn east (right) on West Grand, which turns into Bellevue. To get to Lakeside take Harrison south from West Grand.

**Historic Housewives Marketplace.** Ninth Street between Clay and Jefferson. This is an only-in-Oakland experience, one of the state's first farmer's markets. Whether you're looking for fresh local produce, exotic African foods, fresh seafood, sandwich fixin's, or a couple of Jack's Meats' wonderful sausages, check this place out— even if you're just window shopping. Closed Sundays. (510) 444–4396.

**Oakland Zoo.** 9777 Golf Links Road (off I-580), Oakland, CA 94605. This large zoo at Knowland Park, with a special emphasis on species from the rain forests and African savannas, has a huge array of animals, from lions and tigers to exotic birds and monkeys. There's also a petting zoo and kids' rides, as well as a model of a Kikuyu (African) village. Admission is $6.50 for adults and $3.50 for kids; parking is $3.00. Open daily. (510) 632-9525.

## WHERE TO SHOP

**Jack London Square.** Along Embarcadero between Broadway and Alice, Oakland, CA. This is one of Oakland's premier tourist attractions, with many upscale shops and boutiques, lots of restaurants and cafes with views of the square and/or the waterfront, large hotels with banquet and conference facilities, and a nine-screen movie theater. A highlight is the sprawling **Barnes and Noble** bookstore. (510) 814-6000.

**Marina Square Mall.** In nearby San Leandro on Marina Boulevard (off I-880). A large factory-stores/outlet mall, with the usual suspects: Eddie Bauer, Big Dog, Talbots, and many more. (510) 743-9910.

## WHERE TO EAT

**Shangri-La.** 3336 Grand Avenue, Oakland, CA 94610. Unlike many all-you-can-eat buffets, which feature lots of deep-fried foods and starchy side dishes, this Mongolian-style barbecue specializes in a huge selection of fresh vegetables and lean meats stir-fried while you watch. If you'd rather not assemble your own dish, you can also order off the menu. Lunch and dinner daily. $$. (510) 839-9383.

**Pacific Coast Brewing Co.** 906 Washington Street, Oakland, CA 94607. This lively brew pub, located in an 1870s-vintage building, offers traditional pub grub, salads, pastas, and more. Lunch and dinner daily. $$. (510) 836-2739.

**Citron.** 5484 College Avenue, Oakland, CA 94607. This is one of the East Bay's favorite upscale restaurants, with a menu emphasizing fresh ingredients in French, Italian, and other southern-European dishes, from herbed chicken and mushrooms to innovative pastas. Open for dinner daily. $$-$$$. (510) 653-5484.

**Pizzeria Uno Chicago Bar and Grill.** Jack London Square, Oakland, CA 94607. Specializing in deep-dish, Chicago-style pizza, this is a lively place with both indoor and outdoor (on the Square) seating. Salads and pastas are also available. $$. (510) 251-8667.

**The Fat Lady Bar and Restaurant.** 201 Washington Street, Oakland, CA 94607. For steak, seafood, and a rowdy, good-time ambience, try this Victorian-decorated eatery at Jack London Square. A tradition for three generations. Lunch and dinner daily. $$-$$$. (510) 465-4996.

**Yoshi's.** 510 Embarcadero, Oakland, CA 94607. Better known as a jazz club than a restaurant, Yoshi's also serves some of the best Japanese food in the Bay Area. A virtual institution at its former location on Claremont Avenue in Berkeley, Yoshi's moved to Jack London Square in 1997, increasing by twenty its seating capacity. Thanks in large part to funding from the Port of Oakland and the Oakland Redevelopment Agency, the club was able to sink a sizable chunk into its new digs. In 1999 it was voted Best Bar/Club in a *San Francisco Chronicle* Readers Poll, and regularly books big-name jazz and blues players. Dinner entrees include a wide range of sushi, tempura, and sukiyaki dishes. Open for lunch and dinner daily. $$-$$$. (510) 238-9200.

## WHERE TO STAY

**Waterfront Plaza Hotel.** 10 Washington Street, Oakland, CA 94607. Expensive, but convenient and classy, this large hotel (140 rooms) is right on Jack London Square and offers some rooms with bay views (and balconies). $$$. (510) 836-3800.

**Best Western Inn at the Square.** 233 Broadway, Oakland, CA 94607. Also offering on-Square convenience, this is a smaller (one-hundred rooms) motel/hotel with reliably good service and well-appointed rooms. $$-$$. (510) 452-4565.

SOUTHWEST DAY TRIP 3

San Francisco

## SAN FRANCISCO

A day trip from Sacramento? San Francisco? Sure. If done right, this favorite vacation destination of savvy travelers from around the world, many of whom spend two weeks here and leave still having barely scratched the city's surface, can make for an excellent day trip.

Of course, you're certainly not going to see all the city has to offer, but if you leave Sacramento at a reasonably early hour and time it right (see below), you can be in San Francisco in time for a late breakfast and in time to spend a full day exploring museums, parks, Chinatown, Fisherman's Wharf, and maybe even wandering some of the city's famously diverse neighborhoods.

*A word of caution:* A whole lot of people day trip to San Francisco. And though that means, of course, that you won't be alone, you, well, won't be alone. The difference between them and you? They're all going to work. As the economic and political center of the Bay Area, San Francisco is where the jobs are, and as housing in the city and nearby surrounding area becomes less and less affordable, more people are commuting from farther and farther away. Some will be commuting right alongside you, all the way from Sacramento, while others commute from Sacramento Valley and Bay Area outposts such as Tracy, Turlock, Healdsburg, and Davis. Horror stories abound about folks spending two hours in their cars *each way* every day in order to get to jobs that will pay for the homes they couldn't afford nearer to where they work and can barely afford 100 miles away.

Which means that you should take *timing* into consideration if you're planning a day trip from Sacramento to San Francisco. Though flex-time schedules have spread the commute time out so that the peak hours aren't quite as congested, this has made for a generally longer time that the freeways are still frustratingly busy. Generally, on weekdays from 6:00 A.M. until around 8:30 or 9:00 A.M., most of the major routes into the city are packed, as they are again from 4:00 until 6:30 P.M. or so. Plan your trip accordingly. Weekends are best, when most of the traffic will be going the opposite way you are: San Franciscans leave the city in droves on Friday afternoons and Saturday mornings, to return again Sunday evening. If you head into San Francisco from Sacramento bright and early on a Saturday morning, you'll have the roadway virtually to your own self.

## GETTING THERE

San Francisco is a straight shot from Sacramento, and the 100-mile route is broad, well-maintained interstate all the way. Take I-80 west from Sacramento to Vallejo, where the freeway drops south and follows the east shore of San Francisco Bay. Just south of Berkeley, the road splits, with I-880 continuing south and I-80 banking west over the Bay Bridge to San Francisco, which will deliver you into the city quite near its political heart—City Hall, Civic Center, and the federal and state buildings.

You can also take CA-37 west at Vallejo or I-580 west at Richmond and drop into San Francisco from Marin County. Both of these two routes are longer by maybe a half hour, but they offer the distinct advantage of entry into the city over one of the most spectacular man-made wonders in the world, the Golden Gate Bridge. (There is a $3.00 toll southbound on the Golden Gate, $2.00 westbound on the Bay Bridge.)

*A word on the weather:* No matter the weather in the rest of the state or even in the Bay Area, San Francisco is overcast and/or foggy more often than not. It can be a scorching 90-degree August day across the bay in Marin or Berkeley, and in San Francisco it might be a wet 55 or 60 degrees. Dress for it, or at least bring along clothes to easily change into: sweaters, windbreakers, long pants, etc.

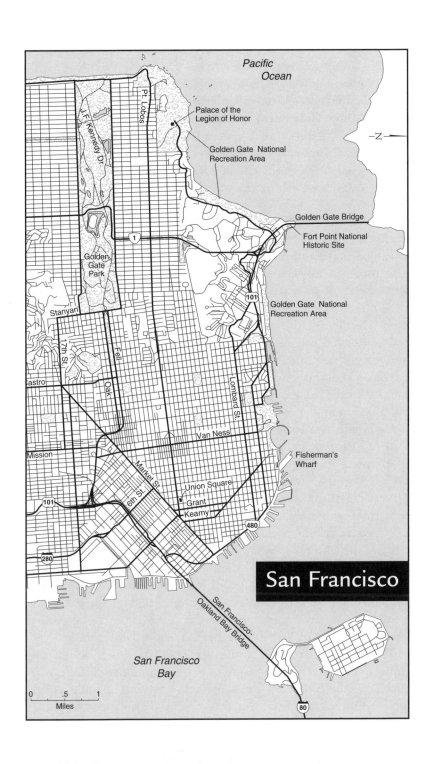

Pacific
Ocean

−Z−

Pt. Lobos

J.F. Kennedy Dr.

Palace of the
Legion of Honor

Golden Gate National
Recreation Area

Golden Gate Bridge

Fort Point National
Historic Site

1

Golden
Gate
Park

101

Golden Gate National
Recreation Area

Stanyan

17th St.

Fell

Oak

Lombard St.

Castro

Van Ness

Mission

Fisherman's
Wharf

Market St.

6th St.

Union Square

Grant

Kearny

101

480

280

San Francisco-
Oakland Bay Bridge

San Francisco
Bay

**San Francisco**

0     .5     1
Miles

80

## WHERE TO GO

Many of San Francisco's best places to visit are known around the world: **Fisherman's Wharf, San Francisco Zoo, Alcatraz, Chinatown, Golden Gate Park, Golden Gate Bridge,** and of course the **cable cars,** to name but a few. And though these are certainly worthy places to visit, having been born in San Francisco and having lived either in the city or within 15 miles of it for the first twenty-five years of my life, I'd suggest a few lesser-known places to see first.

**San Francisco Visitor Information Center.** Inside Hallidie Plaza at Market and Powell, San Francisco, CA. It's easy to feel overwhelmed by the multitude of possible things to do in San Francisco, not to mention by the traffic and the general way the city bustles with activity of every stripe. Not to worry. Just about everything you need to know is available at this information center, which is open daily. Detailed maps, lists of lodging and dining, suggestions for walking tours, call numbers for reserving guided tours, lists of cultural and community events and festivals, as well as helpful folks to answer your questions and point you in the right direction—it's all here. Write the San Francisco Convention and Visitors Bureau at Box 429097, San Francisco, CA 94142-9097. Call (415) 391-2000.

**California Academy of Sciences.** Music Concourse, Golden Gate Park (off Kennedy Drive), San Francisco, CA 94118. This is one of the best ways to spend a day in San Francisco, especially a rainy or cold and foggy one (typical!). Encompassing three separate halls—Morrison Planetarium, the Natural History Museum, and Steinhart Aquarium—this sprawling museum will keep you entertained and educated for as long as you want to stay and as many times as you care to come back. My favorite is the aquarium, in the lobby of which is the famous alligator pit. Beyond these toothy critters are some 14,000 species of fish and other aquatic life forms, from sharks and gars and sea bass to eels and seals and penguins. Simulated tides re-create tide pools, so you watch anemones, crabs, and starfish in a near-natural habitat. Feedings of sharks and other residents occur regularly.

The Natural History Museum is also fascinating, with animal and mineral exhibits from around the world and the distant past, including the Jurassic period. Interactive exhibits include a scale where you can learn what you would weigh on the moon as well as many hands-on children's projects. A highlight is the giant pendulum, which demonstrates the motion of the earth by knocking down a circle of pegs, rotating to meet the ball that swings in place.

Combined entrance fee to the aquarium and natural-history museum, is about $8.00 for adults, with discounts for kids and seniors. Open daily. (415) 750-7145.

The Morrison Planetarium (a favorite for local field-trippers) is the site of a 65-foot dome on the underside of which is projected various perspectives of the night sky, while a narrator provides a lay interpretation of beginning astronomy, from constellations to sunspots, including speculation on the existence of other planets. Small admission fee on top of admission to aquarium and museum. Open daily. (415) 750-7141.

**M. H. de Young Memorial Museum.** Also in Golden Gate Park, across from the Academy of Sciences. In a city of great museums, this is one of the best. In addition to the permanent displays, with emphasis on American painting from Colonial to post-modern, the de Young is also often the site of important traveling exhibits. Shows have included the Mysteries of King Tut's Tomb as well as a recent collection of Van Gogh's paintings. Admission is about $8.00 for adults, discounts for kids and seniors (includes admission to Legion of Honor, see below). Open daily. (415) 750-3600.

**Exploratorium.** 3601 Lyon Street, San Francisco, CA 94123. This is my kids' favorite place to go when they visit their grandparents. They always come away excited about what they've discovered and how much fun they've had, not realizing how much they've learned about science, math, geography, animal behavior, and even themselves. Not just for kids, the museum is perfect for anyone interested in what makes her world the place it is. New exhibits open regularly and are the subjects of much (deserved) excitement. Take Highway 101 south from the Golden Gate Bridge or north from downtown (Van Ness to Lombard) and watch for the signs to the Exploratorium and the Palace of Fine Arts. Open daily. Admission $9.00, $5.00 for students, and $2.50 for kids ages three to five. (415) 561-0360.

**California Palace of the Legion of Honor.** Thirty-fourth and Clement (overlooking Lincoln Park), San Francisco, CA 94121. A replica of the Legion of Honor Palace in Paris and built to commemorate American soldiers who died in World War I, this recently remodeled museum is another of San Francisco's great museums. In addition to the excellent traveling shows that find short-term homes here—from Greek sculpture to French Impressionist paintings—the museum's permanent displays include paintings, tapestries, and sculptures from throughout art history; highlights include paintings by Rembrandt and Monet and a large collection of Rodin sculptures. The large, airy rooms provide excellent viewing areas, while its hilltop location provides outdoor views of the city and great Pacific, sprawling westward. Open daily. Admission fee is about $8.00, with discounts for kids and seniors, and includes admission to the de Young Museum (see above). To get there take Geary west from downtown and go north of Thirty-fourth Avenue. (415) 750–3600.

**Fort Point National Historic Site.** If this massive stone fort, with the south end of the Golden Gate Bridge towering directly overhead, looks familiar, don't be alarmed: If you're an Alfred Hitchcock fan, you've probably seen it before. In Alfred Hitchcock's 1958 film, *Vertigo,* Kim Novak and James Stewart are seen here, waves crashing up along the seawall.

Fort Point was built in 1853 to protect the narrow entrance to San Francisco Bay, and during the Civil War Union soldiers were stationed here to protect the new state from Confederate attack. Today, you're more likely to see wet-suited surfers riding waves toward the rocks and seawall than you are film crews or Union soldiers, although docents dressed in period uniforms lead tours through the fort.

In addition to providing a sense of the city's early history, a visit here offers a unique and fascinating view of the bridge. View up close the massive arched ironwork supports, as well as the south tower, while cars and trucks roll by above and ships sail by en route to foreign ports. To get there follow the signs to the parking lot at the bridge's south end and then take Lincoln Boulevard to Long Avenue and follow it down the hill to the water. No admission fee. (415) 556–1693.

**Ansel Adams Center for Photography.** 250 Fourth Street, San Francisco, CA 94103. The Friends of Photography administer this large complex of exhibit halls, which features not only work by Adams—best known for his dramatic shots of Yosemite—but changing exhibits by other historically important photographers as well as some of the best working today. There's also a bookstore and research library. It's located between Howard and Folsom about 2½ blocks south of Market (Fourth is a one-way street going south). Admission fee is $5.00, with discounts for students and seniors. (415) 495-7000.

**City Lights Book Store.** 261 Columbus, San Francisco, CA 94133. Anyone interested in books and/or San Francisco's literary history must visit this bookstore in the heart of North Beach. Founded by San Francisco's unofficial poet laureate, Lawrence Ferlinghetti, City Lights has been at the vanguard of the city's poetry and literary scene since the 1950s, when regulars included Allen Ginsberg, Gary Snyder, and Jack Kerouac. City Lights still publishes poetry and fiction and offers regular readings and signings. Open till midnight most nights. (415) 362-8193.

**Mission San Francisco de Assisi (Mission Delores).** 3321 Sixteenth Street, San Francisco, CA 94114. Founded in 1776 as part of Father Junipero Serra's California mission project (the only two farther north are San Rafael and Sonoma), this is said to be the oldest building in San Francisco. Characterized by thick adobe walls and rough-hewn redwood roof beams, the mission also features interior decorations imported from Spain and Mexico, as well as a pioneer cemetery outside. Definitely worth a visit, even if you're not particularly supportive of Serra's "mission" to convert the Americans who were here and doing fine long before he arrived. A good way to get there is by going west from downtown on Sixteenth Street to Dolores (3 blocks east of Market). (415) 362-8193.

**Lombard Street.** I know, I know—this is, next to riding cable cars, probably the most touristy thing to do in San Francisco, but, what the hey, if you've never driven down Lombard Street, "the crookedest street in the world," then stopped for the requisite photo-op, you've got to do it at least once. You've seen the pictures, and probably countless slides—maybe even videos—from your relatives' and neighbors' visits. So you know exactly what to expect. Just keep in mind that folks do live on this steep little stretch of street, so be respectful. To get there, take Van Ness (Highway 101) north from downtown. The main part of Lombard continues west at its intersection with Van Ness, while the curly-cue block drops over the east side of the hill. Watch for Lombard between Greenwich and Chestnut.

**Fisherman's Wharf, the Cannery, and Ghirardelli Square.** North end of the Embarcadero. Also unabashedly touristy, but with lots of local color. Unlike many attractions, fabricated to sucker in the unwary tourist, all three of these have long, nontourist histories. Fisherman's Wharf has been the heart of the city's fishing industry for more than a century, and you can still watch hardworking fishermen hauling their crabs and fish ashore. The Cannery was originally a Del Monte processing plant, and Ghirardelli Square—perhaps hard to believe today—was a legitimate factory. Now you'll find specialty shops throughout, ranging from kite stores to jewelers, street musicians and artists (get a caricature drawn to take home with you), and small restaurants and coffee shops. Be sure to check out the **Ghirardelli Chocolate Factory,** where you can watch the world-famous chocolate being made while you try to get around one of their monstrous sundaes or malts. Next to Fisherman's Wharf is the wonderful **Cost Plus Imports** (2552 Taylor), a multistory import emporium selling everything from incense burners to rattan dining sets.

**Pier 39.** Just south of Fisherman's Wharf. This is also a touristy little area, but it's right down on the water, and it can be a lot of fun, and, besides, the views are marvelous. You'll find lots of little shops catering to folks looking for gifts and souvenirs to bring home. You can also book a **San Francisco Bay Cruise,** a tour of **Alcatraz Island,** or hop a ferry over to Tiburon or Sausalito. When you get tired of the crowds, head out to the end of the pier, where you can watch locals fishing, mostly for perch and other small fish, and check out the dozens of seals and sea lions piled onto docks and showing off for the tourists. Another highlight is the regularly scheduled street entertainers—magicians, musicians, and mimes.

Take a five-minute waterfront walk south from Pier 39 to the **Ferry Building,** a true San Francisco landmark. Located at the foot of Market Street, also an important landmark and historical commercial institution, the Ferry Building and the huge clock atop it have been welcoming visitors since the early twentieth century.

## SOME GREAT VIEWS

**The Cliff House.** 1090 Point Lobos, San Francisco, CA 94121. This is a wonderful place to take in the view of the Pacific and to ponder its immensity as you sip a Bloody Mary or Irish coffee, two of the house specials. Built on a large outcropping high above the lapping waves (and barking seals) below, this is about as far west as you can go in San Francisco and is also one of the best places in town to watch the sunset. Lunch, dinner, and Sunday brunch are also served, with an emphasis on local seafood. $$–$$$. (415) 386-3330.

**Top of the Mark.** 1 Nob Hill (corner of California and Mason), San Francisco, CA 94108. Speaking of views, one of the best is definitely that from the glassed-in restaurant and bar at the top of the famous Mark Hopkins Hotel. It ain't cheap, but consider the cost of drinks ($5.00 and up) and cover charge ($6.00 to $10.00 on nights when live music is offered) as the admission price to one of world's most dramatic, 360-degree vistas. (415) 616-6916.

**Carnelian Room.** 555 California Street, San Francisco, CA 94104. Recently voted by readers of the *San Francisco Chronicle* "Best View in the City," the Carnelian Room, fifty-two stories atop the Bank of America Building, offers sweeping vistas from cloud level. Awesome. Again, $5.00 and up for drinks. Dress code: jacket and tie for men. (415) 433-7500.

## SAN FRANCISCO NEIGHBORHOODS

**The Castro District.** Castro Street and surrounding area south from Market to about Twentieth Street, including east to Diamond and west to Church Street. A culturally important part of San Francisco, the Castro is the heart and soul—and represents much of the modern history—of the city's large gay community. Since the mid-1970s, when gays began moving into the neighborhood and more or less claimed it as their own—opening gay-oriented shops, bars, and restaurants, renovating rundown Victorian homes, and instilling in one another a sense of civic pride—this has been one of the most tightly knit and well-defined communities in the city. Thanks in part to the pioneering work of Castro residents, gays and lesbians now make up a large percentage of the city's politicians and other policymakers. In fact, a largely unknown gay candidate surprised much of northern California in 1999 by coming in second, as a write-in candidate, in the city's mayoral race.

**Cruisin' the Castro** has been offering four-hour guided tours of the area since 1990. A recent *Focus Magazine* (published by public-television station KQED) gave the tours four stars; the only other San Francisco tour to earn such a rating was the tour of Alcatraz. The Castro-area tours are $40 a person, including brunch, and are offered daily Tuesday through Saturday, by reservation. (415) 550-8110.

**Haight-Ashbury.** Haight Street east from Ashbury, and surrounding side streets. Ground zero for 1967's Summer of Love, the intersection of Haight and Ashbury was the destination of countless "flower children" from around the world who that summer fled the confines of their parents' homes for the freedoms of the West Coast. Large groups of young people cohabited on single floors in large flats or camped in nearby Golden Gate Park, spending their days strumming guitars on street corners and getting high on mostly innocuous drugs. Rock stars, including the Beatles and the Rolling Stones, came to visit, and others, including the Grateful Dead, the Jefferson Airplane, Quicksilver Messenger Service, Janis Joplin, and Country Joe, all either lived nearby or hung out regularly. Sadly, the era was short-lived. Tour buses even brought gawking visitors to view the "hippies" and "freaks" (who were known to hold up mirrors so that the "freaks" the tourists were seeing were themselves).

The Summer of Love quickly turned into a winter of discontent, however, followed by years of squalor and vice. Hard drugs came to the neighborhood, and with them came violence and serious crime. The myth of free love had dissolved into the reality of hard times on gritty city streets.

Today, the Haight-Ashbury is a bouillabaisse of boutiques, used-record stores, coffee shops, and cafes, aging hippies, businessmen, tattooed nose-ringers, and homeless, heroin-addicted teenagers. Still worth a trip.

For a guided tour sign up with **Haight-Ashbury Flower Power Walking Tours.** Offered Tuesday and Saturday only, the tours depart from the corner of Stanyon and Waller (east end of Golden Gate Park) and cost $15 per person.

**North Beach.** A culturally fascinating and historically important part of San Francisco, North Beach—a roughly triangular area formed by Columbus Street, Telegraph Hill, and the waterfront—was settled largely by Italian immigrants, and the area still is home to small Italian grocery stores and some of the best cappuccino houses in the city. During the 1950s the area was the focus of the beat-poetry movement (see City Lights Book Store, above), and in the 1960s it became internationally famous for its "topless" bars. Now it's a sort of microcosm of the city, where everything and anything goes, a blend of coffee shops, bookstores, taverns, porno movie houses, grocery stores, sex shops, tacky souvenir stores, and dry cleaners. At the same time it's still a hangout for much of the city's literati.

**Chinatown.** San Francisco's Chinatown is defined by Grant Street, the main drag that runs through its heart, from downtown to Columbus, although the district also generally includes Stockton and Kearny, running parallel on either side, as well as Clay and Washington, running perpendicular to Grant. This is a chaotic neighborhood, where Chinese restaurants, souvenir shops, grocers, and other retailers vie for local and tourist dollars, sidewalks are packed, and automobile traffic is often at a standstill. Yet amid all the chaos, there's still an authentic sense of old China. A handful of temples of worship still exist nearby, and in Portsmouth Square, children play and elders chat on park benches, seemingly oblivious to the twenty-first century.

## WHERE TO SHOP

Folks come from all over the world to shop in San Francisco, and one could easily spend months checking out the many shops, from tiny boutiques to huge department stores, from thrift shops to book and music stores. Although some of San Francisco's shopping institutions—such as The City of Paris, a city landmark for much of the twentieth century—have closed down, some remain, and they're great to prowl through, whether or not you plan to make their cash registers ring and their clerks sing.

**Union Square Area.** This is San Francisco's best-known and most upscale shopping mecca, drawing tourists and locals alike, not only to the multistoried shops but to their windows as well, famous for their elaborate decorations. Located in the center of town—between Post and Geary and Stockton and Powell Streets—the square itself is actually a plaza; the stores are on the surrounding blocks. Here are just a few of the Union Square–area shops that are worth checking out: **Macy's,** upscale department store on Stockton at O'Farrell; **FAO Schwarz,** hugely elaborate toy store, kitty-corner from Macy's at the same intersection; **Gump's,** gifts and gadgets, art and antiques, 135 Post Street; **Virgin Megastore,** probably the city's largest collection of music and movies, from CDs to DVDs, corner of Market and Stockton.

Parking near Union Square can be a nightmare, especially if you're trying to find a spot on the street. You'll fare far better in one of the many parking garages, and though prices are steep, the lots are convenient and safe. The **Union Square Garage** is directly under Union Square, and the steps lead right up into the midst of the action (entrance on Geary Street). The **Sutter Stockton Garage** is only a block away, at the corner of Sutter and Stockton Streets (entrance on Sutter).

## WHERE TO EAT

San Francisco is one of the world's great restaurant towns, and one could spend a lifetime exploring the thousands of excellent eateries scattered about the city, from tiny two-table spots in Chinatown to generations-old Italian restaurants in North Beach, from hole-in-the-wall taquerias in the Mission District to exclusive dining rooms on the skyscraping rooftops of the finest hotels. Indeed, many San Franciscans cite dining as high among the reasons they choose to live here—and would live nowhere else, thank you very much. Keep an eye on the San Francisco *Chronicle* Sunday and Wednesday editions, which regularly review city restaurants, old and new. Below is just a sampling of what's available, chosen either for their locations and/or their status as virtual San Francisco institutions.

**Tarantino's.** 206 Jefferson Street, San Francisco, CA 94133. This classic Fisherman's Wharf restaurant has been in business since shortly after World War II, when a couple of San Francisco natives returned from their tours of duty in the navy and converted an on-the-water storage building into one of the city's best seafood restaurants. With views overlooking the docks and the bay, and walls lined with historical photos of San Francisco, Tarantino's offers crab, salmon, abalone, and other locally caught specialties, as well as pasta dishes and fish stews, including an excellent cioppino, and, of course, locally baked sourdough French bread. Open daily for lunch and dinner. $$–$$$. (415) 775-5600.

**Beach Chalet.** 1000 Great Highway, San Francisco, CA 94121. Built in the 1920s and muraled and frescoed in the 1930s as a WPA project, the recently restored beach house is home to a bustling brew-pub-type restaurant at the far west end of Golden Park and overlooking Ocean Beach. Specials include pastas, burgers, salads, as well as grilled seafood and meats. Open daily for lunch and dinner. $$-$$$. (415) 386-8439.

**Mel's Diner.** 2165 Lombard Street, San Francisco, CA 94123. This classic little diner on one of the city's most well-traveled streets offers just what you expect. Burgers, shakes, big piles of greasy fries, and Cokes and malts to wash it all down with. For breakfast: pancakes, huge omelets, eggs-and-bacon-and-hashbrown combos, and good, strong coffee. Open daily. $$. (415) 921-3039.

**Pacific Cafe.** 7000 Geary Boulevard, San Francisco, CA 94121. This small cafe in the Richmond District not too far from the ocean is one of my wife's and my very favorite Bay Area restaurants. Low-key and unassuming, it serves excellent seafood, from swordfish and sturgeon to salmon and sole, and a highlight is the complimentary wine while you wait for your table (no reservations taken). Open for dinner daily. $$-$$$. (415) 387-7091.

**La Taqueria.** 2889 Mission, San Francisco, CA 94114. Given the "Best Burrito" award in 1999 by *San Francisco Chronicle* readers, this little place is the real McCoy. Excellent burritos, of course, but also tacos, and quesedillas, and the perfect ambience in which to enjoy it all. $-$$. (415) 285-7117.

**Gordon Biersch Brewery.** 2 Harrison Street, San Francisco, CA 94105. The best among San Francisco's many brew pubs, this bustling restaurant and taproom serves a bit fancier food than the pub grub you find in most brewery-restaurants. Also, located so near to the city's financial district, the clientele is more likely to be wearing suits and skirts than shorts and backwards baseball hats. Good food, though—salads, pastas, grilled meats, and seafood. $$-$$$. (415) 243-8246.

**Ton Kiang.** 5821 Geary Boulevard, San Francisco, CA 94121. In an area with a disproportionate number of excellent Chinese restaurants, this is, by most locals' estimation, one of the very best in the entire Bay Area. Famous for its soups, dim sum, and vegetable dishes, Ton Kiang is lively and authentic. Open for lunch and dinner daily. $$. (415) 387-8273.

**Boulevard.** 1 Mission Street, San Francisco, CA 94105. In the fall of 1999, Boulevard was given the *San Francisco Chronicle*'s Readers Choice First Place Award for "Best Restaurant," as well as second places for "Best Chef" and "Best Date Restaurant," and third place for "Best American Restaurant." Tough to beat that. Why the accolades? Because the menu has something for everyone, and everything's excellent. Chef Nancy Oakes's specialties range from crab cakes to pancetta to fresh calamari on risotto. Other favorites are the pork chops, filet mignon with chopped herbs and wild mushrooms, and Hawaiian red snapper served with fava beans, sweet corn, asparagus, and cherry tomatoes. Open for lunch and a late-afternoon (2:15 to 5:30 P.M.) bistro-style dinner Monday through Friday, and dinner weekends only. $$-$$$ (415) 543-6084.

## WHERE TO STAY

San Francisco has abundant lodging options, ranging from tiny motels to some of the most elegant hotels in the country. Yet lodging in the city can still be problematic. First of all, some of the least expensive digs are in some of the least desirable parts of town, and in San Francisco, you don't want to try so hard to save money on lodging that you end up in an unsafe part of town. On the other hand, most of the hotels in the better parts of town are very expensive, and in addition to the sky-high room rates, you'll end up paying a lot for parking—sometimes, it seems, as much as you might pay for a room in another town. In addition, even with the abundant lodging options, if you don't have reservations, you're not going to have much luck finding a room. To be frank, when we visit, as much as we like the city, we usually prefer to stay nearby, in Marin or Berkeley, where rates are lower and parking easier, and then drive to the city for the day.

That said, staying in the city is still a marvelous experience. And, though you might pay what seems like extortion rates for parking at your hotel, at least you will be able to park—leave your car in the hotel's lot and use public transportation to get around. Or, better yet, walk. Many of the city's attractions are centrally located and within easy walking distance of one another.

*A word of caution:* Even if you're on a strict budget, don't cut corners on accommodations. Seasoned travelers to big cities know that a motel, hotel, or other inn with a good reputation is worth spending extra for and that trying to save money might mean staying in a place that isn't safe or doesn't feel safe, which amounts to the same thing. San Francisco's a big city, and like any big city, there are parts that are dangerous, particularly at night. Don't try to save a few bucks by staying in an undesirable motel or uncomfortable part of town. Also, make sure that your lodging choice has well-lit parking and twenty-four-hour desk service.

**Seal Rock Inn.** 545 Point Lobos Avenue, San Francisco, CA 94121. Located out in the avenues on the west side of town, far from the craziness of the central districts, the Seal Rock is a classic motor hotel from another era, still close enough to offer convenience without the hassle. Nothing fancy, mind you, but reliably clean rooms and friendly service, as well as an on-site restaurant-diner perfect for a late-night snack or early-morning cup o' joe. Plus free parking. $$–$$$. (415) 752-8000.

**Best Western Tuscan Inn at Fisherman's Wharf.** 425 Northpoint, San Francisco, CA 94133. This is right in the heart of one of the city's busiest and most touristy areas, so it might seem chaotic. But the trade-off is that once you park (for which you'll have to pay), you won't have to worry about driving, and you're within walking distance of scores of restaurants and other attractions. The recently restored (1997) large facility (220 rooms) also includes an on-site Italian restaurant and wine reception every evening. $$$. (415) 561-1100.

**Comfort Inn.** 2775 Van Ness, San Francisco, CA 94109. Also located within walking distance to Fisherman's Wharf and Ghirardelli Square, this is a bit more affordable, if a bit less elegant. Still, good clean rooms and reliable service. $$–$$$. (415) 928-5000.

**White Swan Inn.** 845 Bush Street, San Francisco, CA 94108. This small (twenty-six rooms, four stories) inn about 3 blocks from Union Square offers good-sized rooms decorated with a Victorian elegance. It's also very accessible and convenient, located between Taylor and Mason, with full breakfast and afternoon sherry included in the room rate. $$$. (415) 775-1755.

**Ritz-Carlton.** 600 Stockton Street, San Francisco, CA 94108. Located atop Nob Hill, this is one of San Francisco's two or three most upscale digs, and you'll pay for it. But for a once-in-a-lifetime splurge, or if money is truly no object, this is your best bet. We don't have enough little dollar-sign icons to indicate price, but suffice it to say that rooms *start* at about $300. (415) 296-7465.

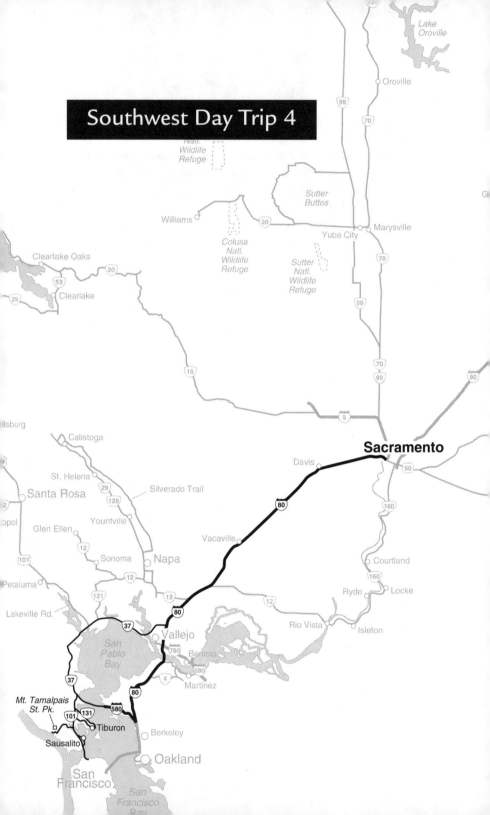

Just an hour and a half from Sacramento, Marin County is a hilly peninsula jutting south toward San Francisco, a short 2 miles away across the straits of the Golden Gate. At one flank the steel gray of the Pacific Ocean seems to roll endlessly westward, while islands and sailboats dot the blue San Francisco Bay to the east. One of the most scenic and culturally fascinating areas in all of California, if not the country, Marin County has long been a haven for artists, musicians, writers, and other visionaries. A Marin hilltop is the site of the last building Frank Lloyd Wright designed, the arresting Marin County Civic Center. George Lucas, of *Star Wars* fame, lives and works in an isolated canyon not far away; in fact, not only are the special effects for Lucas's movies created at his Industrial Light and Magic studios in San Rafael, but most of the cruising scenes from his early film *American Graffiti* were shot on San Rafael's main drag, Fourth Street, with vintage automobiles providing the makeover.

Largely isolated from San Francisco until the Golden Gate Bridge was completed in 1937 (until then they were connected only by ferry), Marin saw a great housing boom in the postwar years, when developers built huge tracts of homes for San Francisco workers seeking solace from the city. In the mid-1960s families bought homes for $30,000 that twenty years later were worth ten times that amount, thanks not only to the idyllic setting but to the proximity to San Francisco's high-paying jobs and world-class entertainment. Presently, the median home price in Marin is $530,000, whereas homes selling for $2, $3, and $4 million are not uncommon. A long-standing local joke is that BMW, the automobile of choice for a disproportionate number of Marinites, actually stands for Basic Marin Wheels.

## SAUSALITO

Sausalito is the southernmost town in Marin, making it the closest to San Francisco and to the Golden Gate Bridge. Originally a fishing village, the tiny town of Sausalito has a definite Mediterranean feel to it: Fishing boats and sailboats rock pierside, and tourists and fishermen alike sip espressos by the water or belly up to the classic little No Name Bar.

Visitors will find plenty to see and do here. An afternoon spent strolling down Bridgeway Avenue, the main street that hugs the shoreline, is a great way to relax and get your bearings, while a visit to the San Francisco Bay Model will provide an instructive overview of one of California's greatest natural resources.

### WHERE TO GO

**Sausalito Chamber of Commerce.** 333 Caledonia Street, Sausalito, CA 94965. A visit here will fill your arms and head with brochures and ideas that will help you make the most out of your visit not only to Sausalito but also to other parts of Marin County. (415) 332-0505.

**Bridgeway Avenue.** This is Sausalito's main drag, much of it winding right along the shoreline with shops across the street, the hillside rising steeply behind them. Grab a bench by the water and enjoy the salty air. Check out the views of Alcatraz and Angel islands, the San Francisco skyline, the Berkeley hills across the bay, and the fishing boats, sailboats, and windsurfers. Mingle with grinning roller bladers, fishermen, and other tourists, and watch a local artist capturing it all with vibrant splashes of color.

**San Francisco Bay Model.** 2100 Bridgeway, Sausalito, CA 94965. This nearly two-acre scale model of San Francisco Bay was designed by the U.S. Army Corps of Engineers to study water flow from the delta to the Golden Gate. Visitors can see how tides work, how river water mixes with salt water, and how development has impacted the

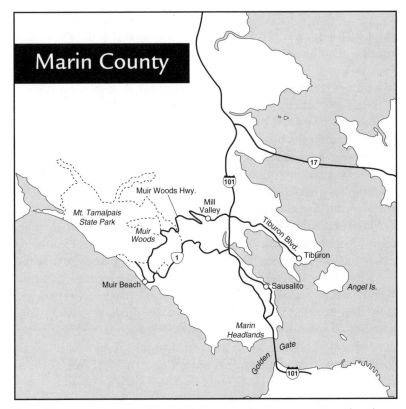

bay. There are interactive exhibits as well as instructional videos. Guided tours are available. No charge for admission. Open Tuesday through Sunday. Memorial Day through Labor Day, Tuesday through Saturday the rest of the year. (415) 332-3871.

**Golden Gate Ferry.** Commuters, sightseers, and tourists regularly share the half-hour ride across the bay to San Francisco's Ferry Building at the foot of Market Street. From there you can walk or take public transportation (ticket is transferable) to Chinatown, Ghirardelli Square, Fisherman's Wharf, North Beach, or any number of San Francisco destinations. Watch for the signs downtown on Bridgeway. Fee. (415) 923-2000.

**Golden Gate Bridge.** Though driving across the Golden Gate Bridge is an experience like none other—especially if you've got a convertible—walking across, at least partway, affords an opportunity to view the magnificence of the bridge and splendor of San Francisco up close and much more intimately. Drive south on Highway 101 and drop down off Waldo Grade through the famous "rainbow tunnels" (rainbows are painted on the south portals), and the view of the bridge and bay and city skyline is sure to take your breath away. Parking lots are located at both the north and south ends, although in summer you might have to wait a while for a spot to open up.

Drive south across the bridge (there's a $3.00 toll) and then circle underneath the on-ramp to the parking lot. From there you can walk up to the bridge and stroll out as far as you want to. You can also drive across, circle under, drive back north, and park in the north-side parking lot, and from there walk back across. There is no toll for pedestrians or bicyclists. Keep in mind that even in summer, the fog and wind get cold; bring a jacket or sweater.

**Marin Headlands.** High above the Golden Gate, and the glittering San Francisco skyline in the distance, the Marin Headlands offers one of the most spectacular views on the planet. A winding road hugs the rugged and rocky cliffside where scattered World War II bunkers look out to the Pacific and hawks wheel on the wind. Turnouts every quarter mile or so provide parking, and benches allow you to sit and enjoy the view. In winter watch for gray whales migrating south and, on clear days, look southwest to the Farallon Islands, a National Marine Sanctuary 27 miles off the coast.

Take Bridgeway south from downtown Sausalito or Highway 101 to the last exit before the Golden Gate Bridge. The road to the headlands will be a steep right.

### WHERE TO SHOP

Sausalito's Bridgeway Avenue is lined with boutiques and galleries, from high-end shoe stores to home-and-garden shops. Many of the galleries feature paintings and sculpture by local artists. **The Village Fair,** 777 Bridgeway, is a three-story "mall" with some two dozen small shops where you can pick up a souvenir T-shirt, a leather jacket, or a hand-crafted coffee mug. *Note:* Sausalito isn't cheap; don't come here bargain hunting.

### WHERE TO EAT

You'll find several wonderful restaurants in Sausalito, many of them with outdoor decks, swooping seagulls, waves lapping at the pilings

underfoot, and even an occasional harbor seal or sea lion popping its head up for a breath and a look-see.

**The Spinnaker.** 100 Spinnaker Drive (at Bridgeway), Sausalito, CA 94965. This is a Sausalito tradition, serving excellent seafood and a wide array of other entrees in a high-ceilinged dining room with huge windows looking out across the bay, or, weather permitting, on a deck over the water. $$–$$$. (415) 332–1500.

**Guernica.** 2009 Bridgeway, Sausalito, CA 94965. Just north of downtown, this is another Sausalito institution (established in the mid-1970s). Specializing in Basque and Spanish food, particularly lamb, they also dish up one of the best paellas in the Bay Area (call ahead). $$–$$$. (415) 332–1512.

### WHERE TO STAY

**Casa Madrona.** 801 Bridgeway, Sausalito, CA 94965. This three-story mansion was built in the late nineteenth century by a rich lumber baron and has been converted and remodeled several times over the years. The thirty-five units are individually deco-rated, some with fireplaces and spas, and offer a luxurious, if pricey, way to stay in Sausalito. Two-night minimum. $$$. (415) 332–0502.

## TIBURON

Tiburon (Spanish for "shark") is a tiny town on a thumb of land jutting from Marin's eastern shore and aimed across the bay at San Francisco. The views are spectacular here, not only of the city's skyline but of Angel Island and slooping sailboats and yachts challenging the always-rough Raccoon Straits that chop at the Tiburon shoreline. Stroll along Tiburon's Main Street, a narrow and colorful single block lined with waterfront restaurants, souvenir shops, and boutiques. Grab a burger and a Bloody Mary on a deck out over the water, watch kids fishing from Elephant Rock, or take the ferry out to Angel Island, where you can hike, bike, or picnic. To get to Tiburon take the Tiburon Boulevard exit from Highway 101.

## WHERE TO GO

**Angel Island.** The largest island in San Francisco Bay, its flanks rising steeply nearly 800 feet out of the water—has been called the Ellis Island of the West. Serving from the turn of the century until 1940 as a "processing" center for Chinese immigrants entering the United States, the island also imprisoned Japanese-Americans during World War II. During the Civil War the island was the site of a Union army fort, currently open to the public. It operates today as a state park, welcoming travelers arriving by the Tiburon-Angel State Park Ferry, San Francisco's Blue and Gold Fleet, or by their own boats—from sea kayaks to 40-foot yachts.

Bicyclists (bikes are allowed on the ferries) and hikers explore the island's camps, barracks, forests, and picnic areas on the 12 miles of trails, and in summer, campers enjoy the handful of available tent sites.

Round-trip ferry rate is about $10 for adults, half price for kids. For information on Angel Island State Park and Ferry, call (415) 435-1915. The number for the Blue and Gold Ferry is (415) 705-5555.

## WHERE TO EAT

**Sam's Anchor Cafe.** 27 Main Street, Tiburon, CA 94920-2531. This is a veritable Marin institution, with excellent food and a lively atmosphere and dining inside and out. Specializing in seafood, Sam's serves breakfast, lunch, and dinner, including a very popular Sunday brunch. Catch-of-the-day can range from local salmon to mahi-mahi to swordfish. $$-$$$. (415) 435-4527.

## WHERE TO STAY

**The Tiburon Lodge.** 1651 Tiburon Boulevard, Tiburon, CA 94920. Offering comfort and privacy, this is one of Tiburon's few lodging options; also within walking distance of the ferry terminal and Main Street. $$$. (415) 435-3133.

# MOUNT TAMALPAIS

Its summit rising 2,604 feet above sea level, Mount Tamalpais affords dramatic views of San Francisco, the Pacific Ocean, and much of the surrounding Bay Area. Hundreds of miles of hiking, riding, and mountain-biking trails weave through ferny canyons, up steep mountain flanks, and across broad, wildflower-laden meadows. Mountain biking was born on Mount Tam, when local cyclists outfitted old balloon-tire bikes with motorcycle brakes and gearing appropriate for steep grades. Atop the mountain is a natural amphitheater, which was modified in a 1930s WPA project into a Greek-style outdoor arena, with seating for 5,000. Each spring, the famous and critically acclaimed "Mountain Play" attracts visitors from around the state and beyond. Past performances have seen "Maria" singing "My Favorite Things" and "Dorothy" belting out "Somewhere over the Rainbow," under perfect skies with San Francisco's highrises sparkling in the distance across the bay. For information on Mount Tamalpais State Park, call (415) 388–2070.

## WHERE TO GO

Drive up **Shoreline Highway/Highway 1** about 3 miles from Mill Valley; then turn north on **Panoramic Highway** and from there onto **East Ridgecrest.** The narrow roads zigzag and switch back for 10 or so miles up the mountain's west flank and climb above the Pacific. Motor homes and vehicles pulling trailers will find it slow going, but there are plenty of turnouts that offer places to rest as well as spectacular views. Continue clear to the top of the mountain (and the end of the road) to the **Mount Tamalpais State Park Visitor Center** and small parking lot. Here you can take in the view of the Bay Area and mountain, not only of the sprawling trails and wooded hillsides but of Marin's reservoir system—little lakes tucked jewel-like among the greenery. Free. The call number for Mount Tamalpais State Park is (415) 388–2070.

**Muir Woods National Monument.** Named for John Muir, the famous nineteenth-century naturalist, explorer, and writer, Muir Woods is a forest of gigantic coast redwoods towering above the oak and eucalyptus on Mount Tam's western flank. You'll find cool, streamside nature trails, where the diverse flora is identified, as well as hiking trails that take you deeper into the forest and higher up the side of Mount Tam. There's a gift shop and visitor center, the starting point for guided tours.

*Note:* Muir Woods is easily accessible from the Bay Area, making it very popular among tour buses and day-trippers. Most visitors, however, don't get much beyond the visitor center. Once you get out onto the trails, the crowds will thin out.

To get to Muir Woods, take Shoreline Highway from Mill Valley to Panoramic Highway, and turn north. After about a mile, watch for the sign to Muir Woods (you'll be turning left). You can also stay on Shoreline nearly to the ocean and then turn right onto Muir Woods Road, which winds back into the park. Open daily. Free. (415) 388-2595.

## WHERE TO STAY

**The Pelican Inn.** Muir Beach Road, Muir Beach, CA 94965. Nestled at the foot of Mount Tam and just yards from the beach, the Pelican Inn is a Tudor-style building with a definitive Elizabethan air, honoring the fact that Sir Francis Drake came ashore not far from here in 1579. Guest rooms and the pub are dark, the tables are of heavy woods, and the shadows cast from the flames from the fireplace dance on thick walls. Perfect for a winter retreat.

Reservations are mandatory, sometimes as much as a year in advance, though if you're lucky, you might be able to call after a recent cancellation. $$$. (415) 383-6000.

The Pelican Inn is also open for lunch and dinner, serving meat pies and other pub fare, especially good when washed down with a Bass Ale or Watneys. $$.

Almost any time of the year, a trip exploring California's world-famous Napa Valley wine country offers a rich bounty of surprises. Whether you're a connoisseur or teetotaler, the wine country is a great escape, the scenery alone is worth the drive. My favorite time of the year is early winter, when the vines have all been pruned back and are not yet in leaf. Straight lines of vines roll mile after mile over hillsides and down into broad valleys, bright yellow wild mustard growing up between them, as the wineries themselves—oftentimes half hidden by winter mists—stand in silent, stately guard awaiting the flurry of spring. This time of the year, you're not as likely to find yourself competing for tables at restaurants or rooms at inns, as most tourists wait until summer or fall to visit the valley.

And summer and fall, too, are magic times, especially fall, when the vines are full and the wineries bustle with the hustle of harvest. Be forewarned, though: Late summer and fall are the height of the tourist season, and the valley gets packed. Best to make reservations for accommodations well in advance; June is not too early to call for a room in September.

The vineyards of the Napa Valley date back to the mid-nineteenth century, when priests from the missions in Sonoma and San Rafael planted imported cuttings on the hillsides and in the valley floor. Little did they know that this naturally ideal climate and soil would provide the means by which their small enterprise would grow into a grape-growing and wine-making industry famous for producing some of the best wines in the world.

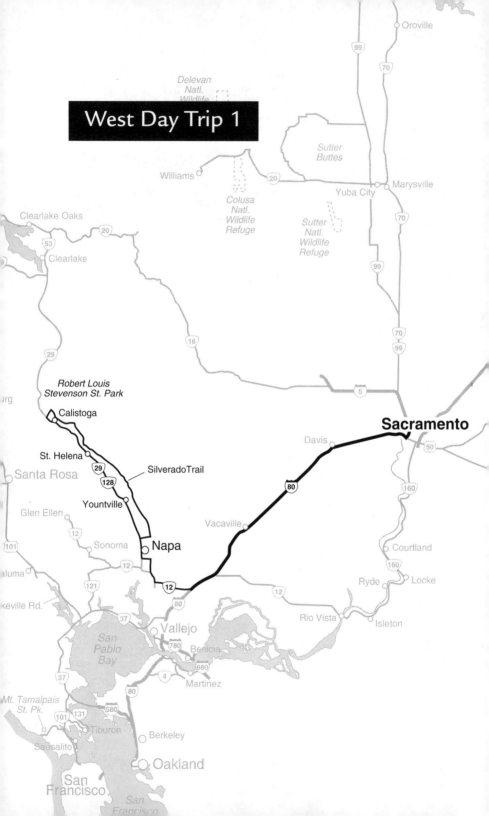

# West Day Trip 1

To get to the Napa Valley from Sacramento, take I-80 west to CA-12; then go northwest to Napa and CA-29 north. The route is well marked.

Napa is at the south end of the valley, along the west side of which CA-29 meanders, through Yountville, St. Helena, and Calistoga. You'll find wineries, restaurants, and inns in all of these communities, as well as scattered between them. Across the valley the Silverado Trail, connected every 8 or 10 miles by a narrow country lane, carves its way along the east side. Here, too, you'll find wineries and vineyards, although most of the tourist facilities—shops, inns, and restaurants—are along CA-29.

## NAPA

Start your tour of the Napa Valley in the small town of Napa (population 55,000), located at the south end of the valley. Though most of the wineries and other points of interest are located north of here, this is a good place to get your bearings.

Established in the mid-nineteenth century by California gold-rush miners, the town has a number of interesting historical attractions often overlooked by tourists in the area for its main attractions: the wineries and wines. In addition to several small historical museums, you'll find a good number of stately Victorian homes, many of them restored to their late-1900s elegance.

### WHERE TO GO

**Napa Valley Conference and Visitors Bureau.** 1310 Napa Town Center, Napa, CA 94559. This is a good place to begin your tour of the Napa Valley, as you can pick up maps, brochures, and other information not only on the wineries, but on historical tours, lodging, dining, and recreational activities from hot-air ballooning to golf. Most useful are the nicely detailed maps that highlight the wineries and indicate the kinds of wines they specialize in. Be sure to pick up a copy of *Stepping Out,* a free magazine highlighting various wineries and showcasing restaurants, with menus and recipes. (707) 226-7459.

**Napa County Historical Museum.** 1219 First Street, Napa, CA 94559. Housed in the early-1900s vintage Goodman Library Building, this museum displays a variety of items of historical significance to the town and valley, from its early farming and mining days through the development of the vineyards and wineries. Call ahead, as hours are limited (generally midday, midweek). (707) 224-1739.

## WINERIES

Most of the following wineries are open daily for tasting and sales from about 10:00 A.M. to 5:00 P.M., often closing in mid-afternoon on weekends. There is usually a small fee ($3.00–$6.00), which lets you taste any of up to a half dozen wines. Drinking water and snacks (French bread, crackers, pretzels) are usually provided free of charge.

**Corodnui of Napa Valley.** 1345 Henry Road, Napa, CA 94559. This subsidiary of Spain's famous Corodnui winery of Catalunya is without doubt the best place to begin your tour of the wineries. Built in and atop a hillside overlooking the vineyards of the Carneros District and the San Francisco Bay to the south, this winery specializes in sparkling wines made with high-tech, state-of-the-art equipment and centuries-old processes. To get there take CA–29 north from Napa. (707) 224-1668.

**Napa Valley Cellars.** 736 California Boulevard, Napa, CA 94559. If you've got a sweet tooth and like dessert wines, this distinctive little winery is worth a visit. Makers of high-quality port (originally made in Portugal in the sixteenth century for English drinkers) from select grapes, Napa Valley Cellars is open for tours by appointment only, although the sales office is open Thursday through Saturday. (707) 257-7777.

**Hakusan Sake Gardens.** CA–12 at CA–29, Napa, California 94558 (take Kelly Road). Located just south of the town of Napa, this is one of the most distinctive breweries in the area, with a capacity to produce more than 240,000 cases of Japan's national drink annually. Made from rice grown in the nearby Sacramento Valley, Hakusan Sake, with a 16 to 18 percent alcohol content, is just slightly stronger than most wines. Traditionally, sake is drunk heated, although some prefer it chilled. Hakusan's twenty-acre property includes sprawling gardens gorgeously landscaped in traditional Japanese fashion. (707) 258-6160.

Other wineries worth visiting in and about the town of Napa include **Saintsbury,** 1500 Los Carneros Avenue, Napa, CA (707–252–0592), Chardonnay and Pinot Noir; **Carneros Creek,** 1285 Dealy Lane, Napa, CA (707–253–9463), Cabernet Sauvignon, Pinot Noir, Chardonnay; and **Domaine Carneros,** 1240 Duhig Road, Napa, CA (707–257–0101), sparkling wines.

### WHERE TO SHOP

The town of Napa was factory-stored in the early 1990s, and there's a medium-sized complex of outlets right along the highway. Stores include those you usually see at these malls: Dansk, Bass Shoes, Samsonite, etc.

### WHERE TO EAT

Although there are all the high-end, stiff-linen restaurants you'd expect (and may have heard of or read about) in Napa, there are also some excellent lower-priced places. A favorite of ours is the **Red Hen Cantina,** 5091 St. Helena Highway (CA-29 frontage road), Napa, CA 94558. Here you can get excellent Mexican food (and margaritas!) for very reasonable prices. Most days are mild enough to allow for outdoor seating on the brick patio. Open daily for lunch and dinner. $$. (707) 255–8125.

**Downtown Joe's.** 902 Main Street, Napa, CA 94559. This classic brewery/restaurant offers good pub fare (burgers, pizzas, grilled chicken) that you can wash down with locally brewed ales and beers. $$. (707) 258–2337.

### WHERE TO STAY

Remember that this whole valley is a major tourist draw and that places fill up quickly. If you're looking for a room between Memorial Day and mid-October, especially, you'd be wise to make reservations at least a couple of months in advance. Some tourists book rooms as much as a year ahead.

**Best Western Elm House Inn.** 800 California Boulevard, Napa, CA 94559. This is a relatively small (sixteen-room) upscale Best Western lodge offering convenience and privacy. All rooms with refrigerators, to chill that Chardonnay. $$$. (707) 255–1831.

**The Chablis Inn.** 3360 Solano Avenue, Napa, CA 94558. A bit less expensive than Best Western, but still nice. Some rooms have spas and kitchenettes. $$-$$$. (707) 257-1944.

## YOUNTVILLE

Yountville, about 10 miles north of Napa on CA-29, is a small town (population 3,500) founded in 1853. It's home to several excellent restaurants, inns, and wineries, including Domaine Chandon, one of the world's leading makers of sparkling wines. Yountville is also the location of the Veterans' Home of California, originally built in the mid-1880s for veterans of foreign wars, as well as a huge nineteenth-century winery that has been refurbished and turned into a mall with boutiques, specialty shops, restaurants, and art galleries. Most of Napa Valley's wineries and vineyards are between Yountville and Calistoga, about 20 miles up CA-29.

### WHERE TO GO

**Yountville Chamber of Commerce.** 6516 Yount Street, Yountville, CA 94599. Stop in here for brochures, maps, and local tips on dining, lodging, and wine tasting. (707) 944-0904.

**Vintage 1870.** 6525 Washington Street, Yountville, CA 94599. This impressive structure, built in 1870 and at one time the home of the largest winery in the valley, offers the visitor the chance to wander through a wide range of specialty shops, many focusing on the Napa Valley wine and California cuisine. In addition, there are boutiques and art galleries, as well as a number of eateries, from espresso-and-pastry shops to upscale restaurants. Open daily. (707) 944-2451.

**Veteran's Home of California.** Situated on an east-facing hillside overlooking Yountville and the southern Napa Valley, this hospital, built in 1884 by and for veterans of the Mexican War and presently operated by the State of California, is not the reason most tourists come to the area. It offers, however, a dramatic contrast to the bacchanalian pleasures and young money nearby—and in so doing provides a healthy perspective to any visit. The home's Armistice Chapel Museum displays a wide range of military artifacts and memorabilia, including photos, weapons, and medals dating from 1883. Admission is free; open Friday and Saturday and by appointment. (707) 944–4600.

**Napa Valley Museum.** 55 Presidents Circle, Yountville, CA 94599. Featuring rotating and permanent exhibits that generally focus on the culture of the area, as well as occasional exhibits from around the world, the Napa Valley Museum is particularly suited to students, with a number of hands-on displays as well as special programs for school field trips. Docents from the museum go out into the local schools and do presentations corresponding to permanent programs and current exhibits. Small admission fee. (707) 944–0500, ext. 201.

## WINERIES

**Domaine Chandon.** 1 California Drive, Yountville, CA 94599. Napa Valley's largest and one of the world's best-known makers of *méthode champenoise* sparkling wines, the winery—owned by the French company Moët-Chandon—is a must on any wine-tasting visit to the area. The fascinating tour offers up-close looks at the centuries-old process and finishes up, of course, in the tasting room, where you can sample their famous champagne-style sparkling wines by the glass ($3.00–$6.00). Tours are free and offered on the hour, daily May through October and Wednesday through Sunday the rest of the year. There's also an elegant, upscale restaurant on the premises (see below). (707) 944–2280.

## WHERE TO EAT

Yountville is home to some of the area's best-known and most upscale restaurants, and, indeed, some travelers come here primarily to experience the incredible dining they have to offer. Be forewarned, though: They ain't cheap. And though most diners claim the food and the overall experience are worth the cost, that cost could run upwards of $200 for dinner for two. Remember, too, that at most of these places reservations are mandatory—sometimes a couple of weeks or more in advance—and even where they're not mandatory, are highly recommended.

**French Laundry.** 6640 Washington Street, Yountville, CA 94599. When folks talk about the best restaurants in the Napa Valley—in fact, about the best restaurants in the country—this little place is almost always part of the conversation. The *prix-fixe* menu generally includes as many as eight different courses, each a work of art often focusing on local ingredients (mustard, rosemary, lamb). Don't plan on a movie, or much else, afterward, as dining here will *be* your evening's entertainment. Open daily for dinner, Friday through Sunday for lunch. Reservations a must. $$$. (707) 944–2380.

**Domaine Chandon.** 1 California Drive, Yountville, CA 94599. Another of the area's fine restaurants with a well-earned reputation, this is the on-premises restaurant of the Domaine Chandon winery, makers of famous sparkling wines. Open for lunch and dinner daily, the restaurant specializes in French and California cuisine with patio dining. $$$. (707) 944–2280.

**Mustard's Grill.** 7399 St. Helena Highway (CA-29), Yountville, CA, 94599. Another of Yountville's well-known and long-standing restaurants, though expensive, is not quite as high end as the French Laundry or Domaine Chandon. The restaurant features a wide range of grilled meats and vegetables, as well as salads and pastas; some of the specials are cooked in the wood-burning oven. Open for lunch and dinner daily. $$$. (707) 944–2424.

## WHERE TO STAY

**Napa Valley Lodge.** 6503 Washington Street, Yountville, CA 94599. This large and upscale lodge in the heart of the valley has fifty rooms, some with fireplaces, spas, and kitchenettes, some with balconies overlooking the nearby vineyards. $$$. (707) 944–2468.

## ST. HELENA

Of all the little towns and communities along CA-29, St. Helena is the one that most feels like a small town, its main street lined with boutiques, restaurants, and coffee shops, but also with shoe stores, delis, and historic buildings dating from the mid-nineteenth century, when vintners first began to grow grapes and make wine in the area. Be sure to allow yourself time to wander the half mile or so that makes up downtown St. Helena, perhaps even stopping for a sandwich at one of the cafes with sidewalk seating—perfect for people watching and enjoying the sun.

## WHERE TO GO

**St. Helena Chamber of Commerce.** 1010 Main Street, Box 124, St. Helena, CA 94574. Maps, brochures, guides to nearby restaurants, lodging, and wineries. (707) 963-4456.

**Napa Valley Wine Library.** 1492 Library Lane, St. Helena, CA 94574. Located inside the St. Helena Public Library, this collection contains some 3,000 works—books, magazines, periodicals, etc.—on grape growing and wine making. Peruse historical documents, reviews of vintage vines, and technical books on grafting and root-stocks. Learn why California wine makers name their products after the grapes they're made with, whereas European wine makers name them after the region where the grapes are grown. (707) 963-5145.

**Silverado Museum.** 1490 Library Lane, St. Helena, CA 94574. Dedicated to the life and work of Scottish novelist Robert Louis Stevenson (*Treasure Island, The Strange Case of Dr. Jekyll and Mr. Hyde*), who honeymooned in an abandoned bunkhouse on nearby Mount St. Helena in 1880. The library's collection of some 8,000 pieces includes first editions, letters (including some from childhood), photographs, original manuscripts, and other memorabilia. Open Tuesday through Sunday; admission is free, donations accepted. (707) 963-3757.

## WINERIES

Some of Napa Valley's best and most interesting vineyards and wineries are within a couple of miles of downtown St. Helena, and within a 5-mile radius of town are probably a dozen excellent ones worth visiting. Best to stop by one of the visitor centers to pick up a map and detailed descriptions so that you can better choose those that suit your taste. That said, though, there are a few that stand out—either for their tours, their intriguing buildings and grounds, and/or the wines themselves.

**Beringer Vineyards.** 2000 Main Street, St. Helena, CA 94574. The oldest and one of the largest wineries in the valley, Beringer makes a wide range of red and white varietal wines, as well as some dessert wines. Most impressive is the huge, seventeen-room Victorian Rhine House, built in the mid-eighteenth century and now housing the tasting rooms and visitor center, and the wine-aging caves, dug by Chinese laborers in the nineteenth century. Open daily. (707) 963-7115.

**Freemark Abbey.** 3022 St. Helena Highway, St. Helena, CA 94574. This smaller, locally owned winery (whereas Beringer, for example, is owned by a multinational corporation) specializes in Rieslings and Cabernets and offers tours and tastings daily. (707) 963-9694.

**Charles Krug Winery.** 2800 St. Helena Highway, St. Helena, CA 94574. Krug, founded in 1861, offers among the best and most popular tours in the wine country. Specializing in Cabernets, Krug is a major player in Napa Valley wine making, and its wines are highly regarded around the world. Open for tours and tasting daily. (707) 963-5057.

## WHERE TO EAT

One of the attractions of downtown St. Helena is the handful of delis and coffee shops, where you can pick up pastries, sandwiches, and other picnic fare to go, not to mention a bottle of wine to go with. In addition, there are a number of excellent restaurants in town, at almost any of which you'll find good food, the menus featuring lots of local ingredients.

**Guini's Grocery.** 1227 Main Street, St. Helena, CA 94574. This is a classic small-town grocery store where you can get sandwiches to go or the fixin's to make your own. Also locally produced wines by the bottle, as well as domestic and foreign beers and ales. (707) 963-3421.

**Tra Vigne.** 1050 Charter Oak Avenue, St. Helena, CA 94574. Located on the east side of CA-29 just a half mile south of downtown St. Helena, this is one of the best restaurants in the area, and though expensive, it's more affordable than some; you can get a good dinner for two, with a bottle of wine, for about $80. Specialties include Tuscan-style grilled meats and seafood and a wide range of excellent pastas, the stone-walled, high-ceilinged dining room providing a casual, European atmosphere. $$$. (707) 963-4444.

## WHERE TO STAY

**Hotel St. Helena.** 1309 Main Street, St. Helena, CA 94574. This small historic hotel is located right downtown and offers the convenience of proximity to the shops and many of the restaurants. $$$. (707) 963-4388.

**El Bonita Motel.** 195 Main Street, St. Helena, CA 94574. About a mile south of downtown, this forty-two-room motel has more affordable rates for this area, while still providing convenience and comfort. $$. (707) 963-3216.

## CALISTOGA

### WHERE TO GO

**Calistoga Chamber of Commerce.** 1458 Lincoln Avenue, Calistoga, CA 94515. This is a good place to get complete information on the range of things to do in the north end of the valley, particularly "mudding" and "hot-spa-ing." Also, information on dining and lodging. (707) 942-6333.

**The Spas.** Folks have been coming to Calistoga since the mid-nineteenth century to take advantage of the famous Calistoga mud—to bathe in the sweet 104°F ooze composed of white clay peat, volcanic ash, and mineral water, and then to luxuriate in a steam bath, whirlpool, and/or warm-water blanket wrap. It's a great way to cleanse both body and soul.

Though many visitors opt to stay the night and enjoy the package deals offered by the dozen or so motels and small hotels in town, day trippers can still take advantage of their wide range of health treatments. And though prices for complete treatments—including aroma therapy, facials, and foot reflexology—can get rather steep, the basic mud-bath-and-steam treatment is quite affordable. For $40–$45, you can get an hour-long mud-bath treatment; at most of the spas, this includes a mineral-water soak and a steam bath.

Most of the spas will be happy to send you brochures detailing treatments and prices, and several of them have Web sites, where you can get additional information. For a full listing of spas, call the Calistoga Chamber of Commerce at (707) 942-6333. You can also get listings and other information at napavalley.com. Just a sampling of the spas:

- **Calistoga Hot Springs.** 1006 Washington Avenue, Calistoga, CA 94515. (707) 942–6269.
- **Calistoga Village Inn and Spa.** 1880 Lincoln, Avenue, Calistoga, CA 94515. (707) 942–0991.
- **Dr. Wilkinson's Hot Springs.** 1507 Lincoln Avenue, Calistoga, CA 94515. (707) 942–4102.
- **Nance's Hot Springs.** 1614 Lincoln Avenue, Calistoga, CA 94515. (707) 942–6211.

**Robert Louis Stevenson State Park.** Located on CA-29 about 8 miles north of Calistoga (at the top of a very steep and winding road). Named for famed Scottish novelist Robert Louis Stevenson, who spent his honeymoon here in 1880, this is an undeveloped (no rest rooms or water) park best noted for its hiking trails up to the top of Mount St. Helena, from which are afforded great views of the surrounding valleys. No charge for admission. (707) 942–4575.

**Old Faithful Geyser.** 1229 Tubbs Lane, Calistoga, CA 94515. As part of the area's massive underground system of hot sulphur springs, this geyser, the largest of several in the area, spews some 60 feet into the air and hisses down into a large pool of mineral water. Eruptions are *mostly* faithful, occurring roughly every forty minutes. Hours are daily 9:00 A.M. to 5:00 P.M. (till 6:00 P.M. during daylight saving time). Admission is $6.00 for adults, with discounts for kids and seniors. Take CA-128 north from Calistoga and watch for the signs. (707) 942–6463.

### WHERE TO EAT

On the short 3 or 4 blocks of downtown Calistoga, there are probably more than a dozen and a half restaurants, all quite good and mostly featuring California cuisine and local wines. You really can't go wrong at any of them.

**All Seasons Cafe.** 1400 Lincoln Avenue, Calistoga, CA 94515. This small corner restaurant is one of the best of the best, serving excellent food at very reasonable prices with an exceptionally friendly wait staff. Specials include pastas, seafood, and chicken dishes, and the restaurant also has an excellent selection of Napa- and Sonoma-area wines, many of which are available by the glass. $–$$. (707) 942–9111.

**Calistoga Inn.** 1250 Lincoln Avenue, Calistoga, CA 94515. A highlight of this restaurant is the outdoor patio, shaded with wisteria and other greenery vining through the overhead trellis. An excellent choice for lunch, especially, the Calistoga Inn specializes in pastas, salads, and grilled meats, as well as local wines and Calistoga-brewed ales and beers. $$. (707) 942–4101.

**Las Brasas.** 1350 Lincoln Avenue, Calistoga, CA 94515. An anomaly in the Napa and Sonoma Valley areas, where California cuisine seems as *de rigueur* as popcorn at a movie, this little restaurant serves some of the best Mexican food—and largest portions!—in the area. In addition to the enchilada, burrito, and taco dishes, you can also get a wide range of stews and chicken specials; try the *pollo boracho* ("drunken chicken"). $–$$. (707) 942–5790.

## WHERE TO STAY

Calistoga accommodations range from standard franchise motels to bed-and-breakfasts to spa resorts featuring mud baths, massages, aroma therapy, and almost any other spa treatment you can imagine, often included in lodging packages. Most of the spas have been in operation for decades, and what they lack in modern construction and polish they more than make up for in comfort and a true sense of tradition.

**Calistoga Village Inn and Spa.** 1880 Lincoln Avenue, Calistoga, CA 94515. This is but one of several motel-spas in Calistoga with a long-standing reputation and loyal customers who return year in and year out. Treatments include mud baths and massages, and the motel also has an outdoor swimming pool and indoor whirlpool, hot-mineral pool, and sauna. Located within walking distance of downtown shops and restaurants. $$. (707) 942–0991.

**Nance's Hot Springs.** 1614 Lincoln Avenue, Calistoga, CA 94515. Another low-key spa-motel that has been in the mud-bath and spa-treatment business for decades, Nance's is located on the north end of downtown Calistoga. A full range of massages and whirlpool treatments is available. $$. (707) 942–6211.

**Comfort Inn.** 1865 Lincoln Avenue, Calistoga, CA 94515. One of the nicer Comfort Inns I've stayed at, this fifty-five-unit motel, a short walk from downtown Calistoga, offers continental breakfasts and convenience, as well as a sauna, an outdoor whirlpool, and a small swimming pool. $$. (707) 942–9400.

## SILVERADO TRAIL

### WINERIES

Rather than heading back to Napa on CA-29, cut east across the valley to the Silverado Trail. This is a much less frequently traveled route, with spectacular views of vineyards and oak-covered hillsides. Most of the two dozen or so wineries along this route offer tours and tastings. The following are just a sampling of the better ones:

**Stag's Leap.** 5766 Silverado Trail, Napa, CA 94559. In addition to the excellent Cabernets produced here, Stag's Leap also makes some of the best Merlot, Pinot Noir, and Petit Sirah, plus some fine whites, in the area—mostly from their own vineyards a half mile north. Open daily for tasting; tours by appointment. (707) 944-2020.

**Chimney Rock.** 5350 Silverado Trail, Napa CA 94559. Specializing in Chardonnay and dry Sauvignon Blanc, this small winery also makes some excellent red wines. Open daily for tasting; tours by appointment. (707) 257-2641.

Though not as well known as the Napa Valley, the Sonoma Valley, just one valley west of Napa, also produces some of the finest wines in the world and offers ample opportunities for exploration and diversion. Whether your bent is visiting the wineries themselves—touring and tasting—or wandering through historical sites, such as Jack London's famous Wolf House and the Sonoma Mission, this is a wonderful area to get to know.

## SONOMA

### WHERE TO GO

**Sonoma Valley Visitors' Bureau.** 453 First Street, Sonoma, CA 95476. A good place to begin your visit to Sonoma and the Sonoma Valley, this visitor center has plenty of information—brochures, maps, books—on everything you need to know about in the area, from wineries to art galleries, restaurants, to local events. (707) 996-1090.

**Sonoma Mission.** On the plaza at the corner of Spain and First Street, Sonoma, CA 95476. This mission, which dates from 1823, is the northernmost of the twenty-one California missions. The mission now houses a restored chapel and a small museum, which displays local historical artifacts as well as items related to the mission movement, including paintings of the other missions. Open daily; small admission fee. (707) 938-1519.

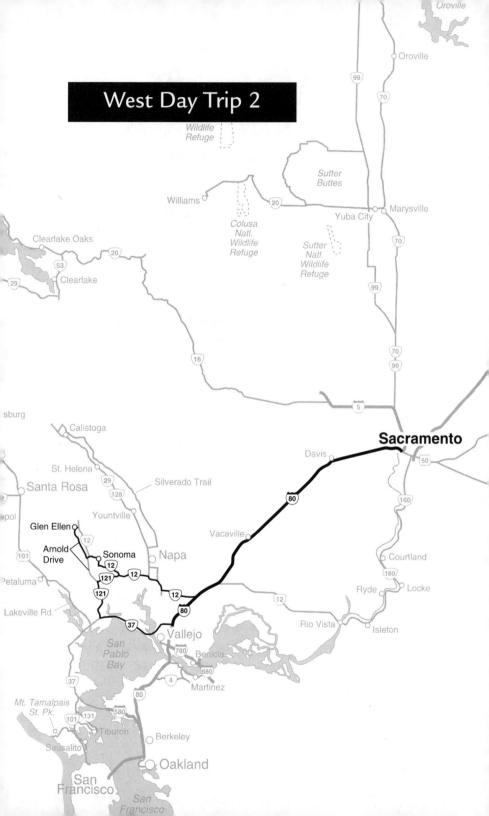

**Sonoma Barracks.** On the plaza at Spain Street, next to the mission, this thick-walled adobe-and-redwood structure was built in the 1830s as headquarters for General Vallejo—in charge of then-Mexico's northern *frontera, Alta California*—and housing for his troops. It also played an important role in the famous Bear Flag Revolt of June 1846, when Yankee rebels, led by Captain John C. Frémont, took more than the town of Sonoma from the Mexicans for two weeks, not knowing that the United States had already declared war on Mexico a month earlier. The barracks houses a museum, with displays on Native American contributions to the area, as well as exhibits from the Mexican and early American periods. Open daily. (707) 938-1519.

## WHERE TO SHOP

You'll want to allow yourself some time to poke around the shops on Sonoma's central downtown plaza. You'll find small wine shops where you can pick up bottles from the wineries in the area, as well as souvenir shops and art galleries representing local sculptors and painters.

## WHERE TO EAT

**Sonoma Cheese Factory.** 2 Spain Street, Sonoma, CA 95476. This is the best place around to pick up picnic fixin's before venturing out to one of the nearby state parks, the picnic facilities at the wineries, or just across the street to the park and playground on the plaza. Watch cheese being made, sample (free) the factory's many varieties (try the jack with pesto), and then have a sandwich made to order or choose a salad from the deli case. You can also pick up crackers, soft drinks, beer, and, of course, wine to complement your meal. Open daily. $. (707) 996-1931.

**La Casa.** 121 East Spain Street, Sonoma, CA 95476. In keeping with the Mexican heritage of Sonoma and the surrounding area, this lively little cantina-style restaurant offers excellent Mexican food and margaritas to wash it down with. You can order house special-ties, combo dishes, or simply plates of nachos and other appetizers. $$. (707) 996-3406.

**Della Santina's Trattoria.** 133 East Napa Street, Sonoma CA 95476. Though there are excellent Italian restaurants throughout the

Napa and Sonoma valleys—and, indeed, half a score or so within walking distance of the Sonoma Plaza—Della Santina is a hands-down personal favorite. We've been going to this small and unpretentious restaurant for more than ten years. Originally located in a tiny corner building on the plaza, it moved down the street in the mid-nineties. Now there's a beautiful patio out back, and as you sit by the fountains and lush greenery, sipping a rich cabernet and munching on fresh French bread, you feel as though you've been transported to a farmhouse restaurant in Tuscany. $$-$$$. (707) 935-0576.

## WHERE TO STAY

**Sonoma Hotel.** 110 West Spain Street, Sonoma, CA 95476. Located on the corner of the downtown plaza, this historic hotel has seventeen rooms, all furnished with period antiques. Offering convenience and comfort, the hotel is within a very short walk of Sonoma's historic attractions and many of its best restaurants. $$$. (707) 996-2996.

**Sonoma Mission Inn and Spa.** 18140 Sonoma Highway, Box 1447, Sonoma, CA 95476. If you want to pamper yourself, this is the place. From the valet parking to the tennis courts, swimming pools, exercise rooms, and variety of spa-and-massage packages, this luxury resort provides one of the great wine country splurges. Located 2 miles north of downtown Sonoma, the inn has nearly 200 rooms, some with fireplaces and balconies, all gorgeously appointed. $$$. (707) 938-9000.

**El Pueblo.** 896 West Napa Street, Sonoma, CA 95476. Probably the least expensive lodging in Sonoma, this little motel still offers clean rooms and convenience—it's about a half-mile walk to the plaza—though it's on a rather busy street corner. $$. (707) 996-3651.

## GLEN ELLEN

## WHERE TO GO

**Jack London State Historic Park.** 2400 London Ranch Road, Glen Ellen, CA 95442. The highlights of this 800-acre park are the ruins of Wolf House, London's 15,000-square-foot stone home, which was torched by arsonists in 1913, just days before the novelist was to move in; and the House of Happy Walls, built in 1919 and now housing a collection of the author's manuscripts, first editions, artifacts from his world travels, specifically art from the South Pacific, and countless rejections slips from publishers. *Note:* Wolf House is a short hike from the parking lot and museum; wear good walking shoes. Open daily; small admission fee. (707) 938-5216.

**Glen Ellen Winery.** 1883 London Ranch Road, Glen Ellen, CA 95442. This small winery offers among the best tours in the area, a tractor pulling a trailer of visitors out into the vineyards, where tour leaders explain the intricacies of wine-making's true beginnings: the soil and the vine. The winery makes good Cabernets and Chardonnays. Open daily for tours and tasting. (707) 996-1066.

### WHERE TO EAT

**Glen Ellen Inn.** 13670 Arnold Drive, Glen Ellen, CA 95442. Just a short walk down the hill from the Gaige House, this little country restaurant is one of our favorites in the area. The high-ceilinged dining room, hardwood floors, and big picture windows make for a cozy setting, and the menu and wine list are superb. Specials often include various pastas, fish, and grilled meats, usually cooked with local herbs and vegetables. Open daily for dinner. $$-$$$. (707) 996-6409.

### WHERE TO STAY

**Gaige House Inn.** 13540 Arnold Drive, Glen Ellen, CA 95442. This is one of the nicest bed-and-breakfasts around, with rooms both in the main house and attached to it, with separate entrances. A highlight is the large swimming pool out back, with the spacious lawn and the creek trickling by. Breakfasts, served in the sunny dining room of this beautifully restored Victorian, are huge and are served at individual tables (or you can join another party at a larger table). All rooms have private baths, some fireplaces and spas. $$$. (707) 935-0237.

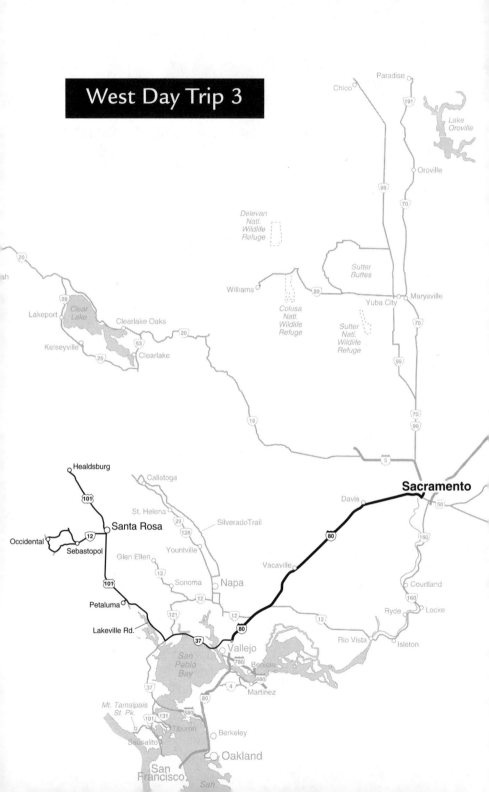

West Day Trip 3

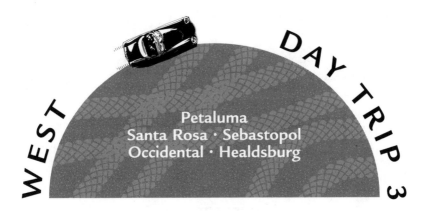

Petaluma
Santa Rosa · Sebastopol
Occidental · Healdsburg

If you're looking to explore an important and scenic region of the San Francisco Bay Area but want to avoid the traffic and chaos of the bigger cities, think about checking out the rural north-bay area and the towns of Petaluma, Santa Rosa, and Healdsburg, which lie along Highway 101 in central Sonoma County. Each has a fascinating history, a pleasant downtown area with shops and restaurants, and plenty of nearby attractions, from wineries to state parks to a French-cheese factory.

## PETALUMA

Petaluma is about a ninety-minute drive from Sacramento. There are several ways to get there, but the best is by taking I-80 west to Vallejo, then CA-37 west (watch for the San Rafael exit) to CA-121. Go north on CA-121 to CA-116, or Lakeville Highway, and go west; this will take you to South Petaluma Boulevard. Go north to Washington Street and turn left (west). This will take you directly to downtown Petaluma.

Petaluma was founded in the early nineteenth century as a hunter's camp and trading center. Later, luckless gold miners came down out of the hills to farm and ranch the area. Among them were a disproportionate number of chicken farmers, and by the early twentieth century, the town had become known as the "World's Egg Basket." The annual Butter and Egg Days celebration in April recognizes the tradition with a parade and festival. In addition, a large number of dairy farmers, many of Italian descent, settled in the Petaluma area—some of the farms west of town are run by fifth- and sixth-generation ancestors of the original farmers.

Recent history includes Petaluma in the movies. *Peggy Sue Got Married* was filmed here, as were parts of *American Graffiti*, its down-home main street providing the perfect 1950s set and its deserted backroads the scene of the drag races.

## WHERE TO GO

**Petaluma Visitor Program.** 799 Baywood Drive (Highway 101 at the CA–116 exit), Petaluma, CA 94954. Start your visit to Petaluma at the offices of this visitors bureau, where you can pick up lists of attractions, from river cruises to antiques shops, as well as maps of self-guided walking tours. Call the offices at (707) 769–0429.

**Petaluma Historical Library and Museum.** 20 Fourth Street, Petaluma, CA 94952. Here you can learn about Petaluma's and the surrounding area's history, including information on the origins and traditions of poultry and dairy farming. Exhibits illustrate Native American life in presettlement Sonoma County, as well as early transportation and architecture, including the unique iron-front buildings of downtown Petaluma and hillside Victorian homes. You can also pick up maps of historical walking tours. Closed Friday. Donations. (707) 778–4398.

**Petaluma Adobe Historic State Park.** 3325 Adobe Road, Petaluma, CA 94954. Built in the mid-1830s, General Mariano Vallejo's huge two-story adobe hacienda was at one time the head-quarters for the original Rancho Petaluma. Now, it's the main attraction of this newly reopened state park, which offers an impressive perspective on pre–gold rush California. Working displays include a blacksmith shop and bread ovens. Open daily. Small admission fee. Take CA–116 7 miles east from Petaluma Boulevard. (707) 762–4871.

**Antiques Shops.** A large number of downtown Petaluma's historic buildings have been converted into shops, many of them specializing in high-quality antiques—thankfully, Petaluma seems to have avoided for the most part the "collectible" (junk) stores. You could easily spend an afternoon wandering through the thirty-one antiques stores in town, enjoying the architecture as well as the

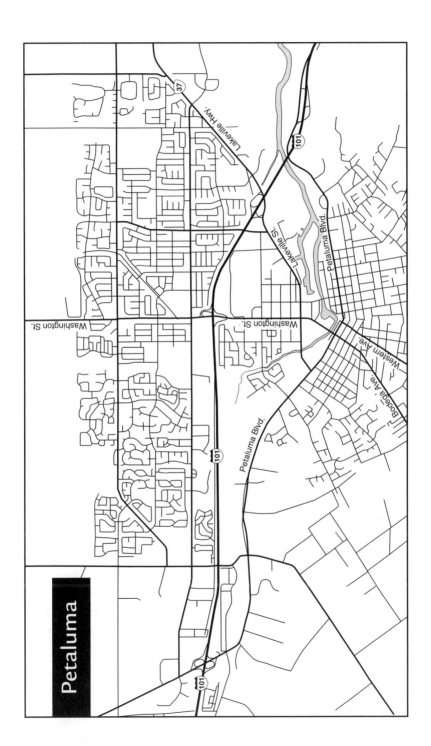

Petaluma

displays of nineteenth- and early twentieth-century dining sets, silver, glassware, and other goods. The Petaluma Visitors Program has a complete list of the town's antiques shops, including a map.

**Marin French Cheese Factory.** 7500 Red Hill Road, Petaluma, CA 94952. Located about 12 miles west of Petaluma—out the gorgeous and winding Petaluma–Point Reyes Highway—this is a surprising little French-cheese factory, where you can pick up picnic makings (there are tables outside beside the large pond) or order from their extensive list of cheeses and cooking accessories. A family operation since 1865 (five generations), the company specializes in French cheeses and sells an assortment of gift packages, including five-pound wheels of Brie and sampler sets in attractive wooden boxes, which come with recipes and suggestions for serving. Even if Brie and Camembert aren't your thing, the drive out alone is highly recommended, especially in spring, when the hillsides are green, the creeks trickle with winter runoff, and wildflowers paint the meadows. Open daily. (707) 762-6001.

### WHERE TO EAT

**The Apple Box.** 224 B Street, Petaluma, CA 94952. This little place down on the river is simply one of the best coffee shops in the north bay. Get the house blend or a latte or a big cup of steaming breakfast tea, and choose from a sinful array of baked goods, from croissants to scones to muffins. A great place to jump-start your Petaluma day. There's also kitchenware for sale. $. (707) 762-5222.

**New Marvin's.** 145 Kentucky Street, Petaluma, CA 94952. For a more traditional breakfast—pancakes, eggs, etc.—try this longtime local hangout right downtown. New Marvin's also serves lunch, including soups, sandwiches, and salads. $$. (707) 765-2371.

**Dempsey's Restaurant and Brewery.** 50 East Washington, Petaluma, CA 94952. Located on the river right near the footbridge, Dempsey's serves up some of the best food in town. The lunch menu includes burgers, fish and chips, and other traditional ale-house grub ($-$$), whereas the dinner menu is more upscale, featuring California cuisine with rotating specialties, usually including pastas, fish, chicken, and beef. $$-$$$. (707) 765-9694.

**Volpi's Ristorante and Bar.** 122 Washington, Petaluma, CA 94952. This classic family-style Italian restaurant has been serving

Petalumans and passers-through for generations (the back room was a speakeasy in the 1920s). Whether you go for the lasagna, the veal parmigiana, or the spaghetti in marinara sauce, you won't be disappointed. Closed Mondays. $$–$$$. There's also a deli, where you can get sandwiches to go. $. (707) 765-0695.

**McNear's Saloon and Dining House.** 23 North Petaluma Boulevard, Petaluma, CA 94952. A great local after-work hangout, McNear's is a lively downtown restaurant with a huge range of microbrews on tap and several large-screen televisions always tuned to sports. Chase your Petaluma Pale with a burger, salad, or pasta dish. $$. (707) 765-2121.

**Sonoma Taco Shop.** 953 Lakeville Highway, Petaluma, CA 94952. This is one of a small chain of north-bay taquerias that have proved immensely popular among connoisseurs of good Mexican food. The burritos, tacos, and enchiladas are all excellent and can be ordered to go or to eat in the small lobby. $. (707) 778-7921.

## WHERE TO STAY

**Cavanaugh Inn.** 10 Keller Street, Petaluma, CA 94952. Just a block from downtown Petaluma, this beautifully restored Victorian offers seven rooms, all decorated with period furnishings. $$–$$$. (707) 765-4657.

**Best Western Petaluma Inn.** 200 South McDowell (corner of Washington), Petaluma, CA 94954. For more conventional motel accommodations, this is a good bet: convenient, with seventy-five clean, good-sized rooms, reasonably priced. $$–$$$. (707) 763-0994.

# SANTA ROSA

Continue up Highway 101 about 18 miles to Santa Rosa, the largest town in Sonoma County and one of the fastest-growing communities in the Bay Area. Founded in the nineteenth century, Santa Rosa was largely flattened in the 1906 earthquake, more famous for destroying San Francisco. Much of historical Santa Rosa has also been lost to urban renewal, and unfortunately the city now draws more people to its huge shopping mall and "auto centers" than to its off-beat little shops and museums, which are there for visitors who look beyond the banners of the Toyota-Dodge-Mazda-Lexus-Ford-Nissan-Jeep dealer.

Santa Rosa native sons include Luther Burbank, the experimental horticulturalist; Robert Ripley, who launched his "Believe It or Not!" syndication here; and Charles Schulz, whose "Peanuts" cartoon ran for nearly fifty years in as many as 2,600 newspapers around the world until his retirement in January 2000.

## WHERE TO GO

**Sonoma County Visitors Bureau.** 2300 County Center Drive, Suite B260, Santa Rosa, CA 95403. Pick up maps and brochures, including lots of information on touring and tasting at Sonoma County wineries. (707) 565-2146.

**Greater Santa Rosa Convention and Visitors Bureau.** 9 Fourth Street, Santa Rosa, CA 95401. Located right downtown at Railroad Square. Get visitors guides with complete listings of lodging, dining, and exploring Santa Rosa and beyond. (707) 577-8674.

**Sonoma County Museum.** 425 Seventh Street, Santa Rosa, CA 95401. With rotating exhibits on the area's history, culture, and arts, this museum offers a good overview of Santa Rosa, from its beginnings as a farming community through the twenty-first century as a center for north-bay commerce. Open Wednesday through Sunday; small admission fee. (707) 579-1500.

**Luther Burbank Home and Gardens.** Santa Rosa and Sonoma Avenues, Santa Rosa, CA 95401. A real treat for gardeners and other fans of flora, this museum honors Luther Burbank (1849–1926), who studied with Darwin and was friends with Jack London, Henry Ford, William Jennings Bryan, and many other important people of the time. Burbank, who "created" many of the plants and flowers we know at present—from the Shasta daisy to the giant calla lilly—deeply offended more conservative thinkers, who thought abhorrent his advocation of eugenics. His home and gardens, now a National Historic Landmark, are open to the public, who can visit the greenhouse where he conducted his experiments and can view the many plants he introduced. The gardens are open daily year-round (free), and the home and other buildings are open Tuesday through Sunday, April through October (small fee). (707) 524-5445.

**Robert L. Ripley Memorial Museum.** 492 Sonoma Avenue, Santa Rosa, CA 95401. View the three-headed calf, carrots that grow upside down, a Labrador retriever that can play the "Star Bangled Banner" on the oboe. Well, not really. But you can visit the "Church of One Tree," a church (including a 70-foot spire) that was built in 1875 from a single coast redwood tree. The museum also displays artifacts from Ripley's life, original "Believe It or Not!" comic strips, and exhibits from Santa Rosa's past. (707) 524-5233.

**Redwood Empire Ice Arena.** 1667 West Steele Lane, Santa Rosa, CA 95403. Owned and operated by "Peanuts" creator, Santa Rosan Charles Schulz, this 85- by 185-foot ice rink is open to the public for open skating, lessons, birthday parties, competitive skating, hockey tournaments, and special occasions, including an annual Christmas show, with nationally known skaters. (707) 546-7147.

**Snoopy's Gallery and Gift Store.** 1665 West Steele Lane (adjacent to the arena), Santa Rosa, CA 95403. As much a part of American culture as Huck Finn and Tom Sawyer, Charles Schulz's characters—Lucy, Charlie Brown, Linus, and the rest—live on in a two-story gift shop and museum, which exhibits Schulz' awards, photographs, and original drawings. Schulz wrote the "Peanuts" comic strip from his home in Santa Rosa and donated many of the items. Open daily. (707) 546-3385.

**Sonoma County Farm Tours.** Box 6032, Santa Rosa, CA 95406. Take a self-guided tour of as many as one hundred local farms in and around Santa Rosa. Depending on the season you might visit apple or pear farms, vineyards, or others all in full operation. Write or call for a map, or stop by the Sonoma County Visitors Bureau. (707) 586-8100.

## WHERE TO EAT

**Lisa Hemenway's Bistro.** 714 Village Court (Farmers Lane at Sonoma Avenue), Santa Rosa, CA 95405. Recipient of several Awards of Excellence from *Wine Spectator* magazine, this is generally regarded as the best restaurant in Santa Rosa and one of the best restaurants in the entire north bay. Hemenway characteristically uses fresh local ingredients in innovative combinations to achieve a California cuisine influenced by her world-wide travels. Try a Thai martini—vodka with lemon grass and ginger—and the coq au vin with wild mushrooms. Open Monday through Saturday for lunch and dinner. $$–$$$. (707) 526–5111.

**John Ash and Company.** 4330 Barnes Road, Santa Rosa, CA 95403. This is one of Sonoma County's best known and most upscale restaurants, with a well-deserved reputation for innovative cuisine—California-style with world-wide influences, particularly from Asia and the Mediterranean. Located at the Vintner's Inn (see below), this restaurant offers a large selection of Sonoma, Napa, and Anderson Valley wines, as well as wines from other parts of California and Europe. $$$. (707) 527–7687.

**Third Street Aleworks.** 610 Third Street, Santa Rosa, CA 95404. Located right downtown, this brewery and restaurant serves salads, pastas, burgers, and sandwiches, as well as grilled meats and daily specials. Open daily for lunch and dinner. $$. (707) 523–3060.

## WHERE TO STAY

**Gables Inn.** 4257 Petaluma Hill Road, Santa Rosa, CA 95404. This highly reputed bed-and-breakfast, located on three acres about 4 miles from downtown Petaluma, offers eight guest rooms, including the separate cottage, which has its own spa and kitchenette. The rooms are all elaborately decorated, and the many returning guests all have their own favorites. $$$. (707) 585–7777.

**Hotel La Rose.** 308 Wilson Street, Santa Rosa, CA 95401. Offering a bit of what remains of historic Santa Rosa, this three-story cobblestone structure was built in 1907. Located downtown on Railroad Square, it also provides access to downtown shopping and to the numerous coffee shops and restaurants on the square. $$–$$$. (707) 579–3200.

**Hillside Inn Motel.** 2901 Fourth Street, Santa Rosa, CA 95409. A classic: inexpensive, convenient, clean, with friendly staff and an adjoining coffee shop. Also, some rooms have kitchenettes. $$. (707) 546–9353.

**Holiday Inn Express.** 870 Hopper Avenue (Hopper Avenue exit from Highway 101), Santa Rosa, CA 95403. These downscaled (no restaurants) versions of classic Holiday Inns are reliably clean, quiet, and efficient. If all you're doing is pulling off the road before heading out tomorrow, you can't go wrong here. $$. (707) 545–9000.

**Flamingo Resort Motel.** 2777 Fourth Street, Santa Rosa, CA 95405. Offering 136 rooms, tennis courts, a health-and-fitness center, whirlpools, and an Olympic-size swimming pool, this attractive ten-acre resort and spa is a great place to base yourself for a tour of Sonoma County. Very reasonably priced considering the amenities. $$–$$$. (707) 545–8530.

**Vintner's Inn.** 4350 Barnes Road, Santa Rosa, CA 95403. Located on forty-five acres and surrounded by vineyards, this European-style resort hotel is perfect for that splurge or special occasion. The forty-four rooms are all very nicely appointed, and many open onto the central courtyard. Adjacent is the nationally acclaimed John Ash and Company restaurant (see above). $$$. (707) 575–7350.

## SEBASTOPOL

Seven miles west of Santa Rosa on CA-12, this little town is worth a side trip if you can spare a couple of hours. This is one of the country's premier apple-growing areas, with rolling hills of orchards, most notably the Gravensteins, and annual fairs and special events honoring the apple and its contribution to local commerce.

### WHERE TO GO

**Sebastapol Chamber of Commerce.** 265 Main Street, Sebastopol, CA 95472. Stop in here for information on the annual Apple Blossom Fair, as well as on lodging and dining and other attractions in the area. (707) 823–3032.

### WHERE TO EAT

**Powerhouse Brewing Company.** 268 Petaluma Avenue, Sebastopol, CA 95472. One of the best microbreweries in Sonoma County, this pub and restaurant serves burgers, fish, and chicken dishes, as well as salads and pastas. Open Wednesday through Sunday for dinner, Friday through Sunday for lunch. $$–$$$. (707) 829–9171.

## WHERE TO STAY

**Gravenstein Inn.** 3160 Hicks Road, Sebastopol, CA 95472. A gorgeous 1872 farmhouse (a National Historic Landmark) converted into a bed-and-breakfast, this inn offers four upstairs rooms (two with shared bath), all nicely private. There's also a swimming pool as well as an apple orchard on the six-acre property. $$-$$$. (707) 829-0493.

**Holiday Inn Express and Suites.** 1101 Gravenstein Highway, Sebastopol, CA 95472. This brand-new lodge (spring 1998) offers eighty-two rooms ranging from economy units to decent-sized suites. $$-$$$. (707) 829-6677.

## OCCIDENTAL

Even farther out of your way than Sebastopol, but definitely worth a visit, is this unique little town nestled among the redwoods of the coastal mountains. When I was a kid, we always called Occidental "the restaurant town," as that's virtually all that's there. And going to Occidental to eat is about the only reason to go there. I remember one Mother's Day afternoon in, oh, probably 1963 or so, when we'd been out for a jaunt in the Plymouth wagon, my dad's mother along for the ride. Sometime in mid-afternoon, Pop decided on a lark to take Grandma and the family to dinner in Occidental. Big mistake. Traffic was bumper-to-bumper for miles outside the little town, as folks from around Sonoma and Marin Counties descended on Occidental to treat their mothers and grandmothers to dinner. We finally made it, knowing it was worth the trouble, and by the time the soup was served at the Union Hotel, even my two little brothers, who had grown quite cranky, were wearing big smiles.

To get to Occidental take CA-116 north about 3 miles from Sebastopol to Graton and go west on Graton Road 5½ miles. You can also continue west from Sebastopol on the Bodega Highway about 6 miles and then take Bohemian Highway north about 4 miles to Occidental. Road signs indicate the way.

## WHERE TO EAT

**Union Hotel.** 3731 Main Street, Occidental, CA 95465. One of my all-time favorite places to eat, this unpretentious restaurant, in a renovated early twentieth-century hotel, serves excellent family-style dinners at very reasonable prices. The huge, picnic-style tables are covered with red-and-white tablecloths, anchored with a chianti-bottle-in-a-basket. Entrees include chicken, beef, and excellent pastas, each of which includes soup, salad, beans, potatoes, and dessert. $$–$$$. (707) 874-3444.

# HEALDSBURG

About 15 miles north of Santa Rosa on Highway 101, Healdsburg has recently transformed itself from a sleepy farming community to a bustling home for professionals and young families who have fled the Bay Area's madness and higher cost of living. Founded as a trading post on the Russian River, Healdsburg takes advantage of its location near some of the best wine-growing country in the world and serves as a jumping-off point for folks exploring the Alexander, Dry Creek, and Russian River valleys. Healdsburg's central plaza—which has a similar Spanish look and feel to Sonoma's—is a cheerful shopping and dining area, with several wine-tasting rooms operated by local wineries as well as plenty of park benches perfect for people watching. If you're lucky, you might even get to hear free live music from the plaza's gazebo.

## WHERE TO GO

**Healdsburg Chamber of Commerce and Visitors Center.** 217 Healdsburg Avenue, Healdsburg, CA 95448. Located on the main route between the Highway 101 exit to Healdsburg and the downtown plaza, this is a good place to begin your exploration of the town. Pick up everything from relocation guides to brochures for bed-and-breakfasts to maps of historical walking tours and to nearby wineries. Open daily. (707) 433-6935.

**Downtown Plaza.** Don't pass up the opportunity to stroll around the little downtown plaza, the hub of Healdsburg. On a nice day restaurants serve at little sidewalk tables, and locals and tourists alike window shop and rest on the benches placed in front of almost every shop. Sample local wines at several wine-tasting shops.

**Healdsburg Museum.** 221 Matheson Street, Healdsburg, CA 95448. Illustrating Healdsburg's and the county's past from prehistoric through modern times, this museum displays Pomo (local Native American) basketry, saddles once owned by Kit Carson (who spent time trapping nearby), and more than 5,000 newspaper clippings and photographs dating from 1865.

**Healdsburg-area Wineries.** Like much of the Sonoma and Napa valley areas, wineries seem to be just about everywhere around here, and one could spend weeks, if not months, visiting the tasting rooms and touring the processing plants and vineyards. A few stand out, though, and are worth special visits: **Pezzi King Tasting Room and Gardens,** 3805 Lambert Bridge Road, Healdsburg, CA 95448 (707-431-9388), a gorgeous outdoor area shaded by redwoods; **Preston Vineyards,** 9282 West Dry Creek Road, Healdsburg, CA 95448 (707-433-3372), specializing in ports and cabernets, as well as fresh, wood-fired bread with the tasting; and **J. Rochioli Vineyards and Winery,** 6192 Westside Road, Healdsburg, CA 95448 (707-433-2305), generations-old winery with excellent chardonnays and pinot noirs; **Simi Winery,** 17275 Healdsburg Avenue, Healdsburg, CA 95448 (707-433-6981), owned by Moët-Hennesey of France; very nice stone-and-redwood tasting room.

**Lake Sonoma Recreation Area.** Dry Creek Road (11 miles west of downtown), Healdsburg, CA 95448. This 18,000-acre recreation area on 3,600-acre Lake Sonoma offers camping, swimming, boating, windsurfing, fishing, hiking, and horseback riding. There's also a fish hatchery and a visitor center, with Native American displays and exhibits of local wildlife. (707) 433-9483.

### WHERE TO EAT

You'll find lots of nice little restaurants right on and near the downtown plaza, many with patio seating.

**Bear Republic Brewing Company.** 345 Healdsburg Avenue, Healdsburg, CA 95448. This is Healdsburg's version of the ubiquitous brew pub, featuring beers and ales made on the premises and good, solid pub grub—salads, burgers, pastas, sandwiches. $$. (707) 433-2337.

**Bistro Ralph.** 109 Plaza Street, Healdsburg, CA 95448. A local favorite, looking directly out at the plaza, this little restaurant specializes in California cuisine using local ingredients, from grilled portobello mushrooms to salads and pasta dishes. Dinner daily, lunch weekdays. $$-$$$. (707) 433-1380.

**Lotus Thai.** 109A Plaza Street, Healdsburg, CA 95448. For good Thai food—noodles in peanut sauce, grilled chicken with hot peppers—try this little place right next door to Bistro Ralph. Closed Monday. $$. (707) 433-5282.

**Oakville Grocery.** 124 Matheson Street, Healdsburg, CA 95448. A wine-country classic, this marketplace and deli serves pizzas, sandwiches, and salads—take out or eat in. On nice days the outdoor patio, looking across to the plaza, is open for dining. Open daily. $$. (707) 433-2300.

**Tamale Malone's.** 245 Healdsburg Avenue, Healdsburg, CA 95448. This colorful little Mexican restaurant specializes in veggie burritos, papaya salads, and, of course, tamales. There's also a lively bar, with creative tequila and other drinks. $-$$. (707) 431-1856.

**Cousteaux French Bakery.** 417 Healdsburg Avenue, Healdsburg, CA 95448. Located just a couple of blocks north of the downtown plaza, this little bakery carries a huge assortment of fresh breads and pastries, including croissants, bear claws, and muffins, as well as gourmet coffees. Food and drink to go or to savor on the premises. Open daily. $. (707) 433-1913.

## WHERE TO STAY

**Haydon Street Inn.** 321 Haydon Street, Healdsburg, CA 95448. Imagine my wife's and my delight when we opened a Christmas gift from my parents one year and found a gift certificate to the Haydon Street Inn (including child- and dogsitting—thanks, Mom and Dad!). A perfect getaway, within walking distance to the plaza, the early twentieth-century Queen Anne is one of the nicest among Healdsburg's many very nice bed-and-breakfasts. $$$. (707) 433-5228.

**Madrona Manor.** 1001 Westside Road (P.O. Box 818), Healdsburg, CA 95448. This in another of Healdsburg's bed-and-breakfasts in a restored Victorian, all eighteen rooms with fireplaces. In addition to the full breakfast included in the rates, the kitchen serves first-rate dinners in the inn's three elegant dining rooms, emphasizing local wines, and foods to complement them. There's also a large swimming pool, unusual for a bed-and-breakfast inn. $$$. (707) 433-4231.

**Best Western Dry Creek Inn.** 198 Dry Creek Road, Healdsburg, CA 95448. Amenities here include a fitness room, pool, and spa, and each of the 102 rooms comes with a gift bottle of local wine. Free continental breakfast. $$. (707) 433-1129.

**Vineyard Valley Inn.** 178 Dry Creek Road, Healdsburg, CA 95448. This is a much smaller facility (twenty-three rooms) just down the road, also offering convenience and dependable service, as well as a free continental breakfast. $$. (707) 433-0101.

**Clear Lake**
**Ukiah · Boonville**

This meandering tour northwest from Sacramento takes you on almost every kind of roadway and through a surprisingly diverse landscape. You'll zip through valley farmland, wind over cattle- and sheep-dotted foothills, climb up into the Coast Range, drop down into the Clear Lake basin, and gradually lift up into the green and often-foggy coastal forests. Take I–5 north about 15 miles to Woodland and the junction with CA–16, which you'll take northwest about 40 miles to CA–20. This is one of the most frequently well-traveled east-west routes in the northern part of the state, with folks from throughout the valley using it to get to the coast, to campgrounds, RV parks, and the many resorts and fishing villages that dot the coast from Fort Bragg south to Jenner. You won't follow it all the way to the coast, though: At CA–20 and Highway 101, you'll go south through Ukiah and then take CA–253 west to Boonville. From there you can either return to Sacramento the way you came or continue south on CA–128 through Cloverdale, Calistoga, and St. Helena (also CA–29), continue to Napa, and then go back to Sacramento on I–80 east.

## CLEAR LAKE

California's largest natural freshwater lake, with a 70-mile shoreline, Clear Lake has been a tourist destination for centuries, actually for millennia: Long before the Pomo Indians settled in the area, prehistoric people lived here, and petroglyphs 10,000 years old have been

# Northwest Day Trip 1

discovered nearby. During the early part of the century, it was the site of many wineries and taverns, which closed down during Prohibition and never re-opened. At present it's a very *un*ritzy resort area, with shoreline motels and cottages, many in need of paint and repair, catering to fishers and working folk. For all that, though, it's also refreshingly free of the upscale boutiques and trendy cafes so pervasive in most tourist areas. Instead, you'll find bait shops, mini-storage yards (for fishing boats and RVs), and video-rental stores. Recently, wineries have begun to resurface in the area, some of which are already giving nearby Napa and Sonoma wineries runs for their money.

## WHERE TO GO

At the little community of **Clearlake Oaks,** you'll find a couple of small restaurants, a grocery store, and a post office. From there you can take a side trip to the town of **Clearlake** (about 4 miles south of CA-20 on CA-53). Another fishing and resort community, Clearlake has recently begun to experience a bit of a rebirth, with new homes under construction and other development actually creating a need for traffic lights and other symbols of civilization.

If you want, you can continue from there (on CA-29) around the west side of the lake, through **Kelseyville** and **Lakeport,** hooking back up with CA-20 at the little community of **Upper Lake.** Otherwise, continue west on CA-20 from Clearlake Oaks through **Lucerne, Nice,** and **Upper Lake.**

**Lake County Visitors Information Center.** 875 Lakeport Boulevard Lakeport, CA 95453. The friendly folks here will happily fill your arms with all kinds of information on the area, from dining and lodging facilities to fishing tournaments and wineries. (707) 263-9544.

**Clearlake State Park.** 5300 Soda Bay Road, Kelseyville, CA 95451. This 500-acre park on the lake's west shore offers camping, boating, fishing, and hiking, with marked natural trails winding through the oaks and cottonwoods (watch out for poison oak). The visitor center displays the lake's natural history through dioramas and videos. Small admission fee. (707) 279-4293.

## WHERE TO STAY

**Konocti Harbor Resort and Spa.** 8727 Soda Bay Road, Kelseyville, CA 95451. Though troubled in recent years by a series of legal problems, some of which prompted temporary closing, Konocti Harbor has steadfastly and resolutely been at the vanguard of Clear Lake's modern resorts. Best known for its concerts, which are part of lodging packages, the resort has attracted big-name acts from Merle Haggard and Clint Black to the Beach Boys and the Righteous Brothers. Lodging (250 rooms, many with kitchenettes) is relatively inexpensive, and facilities include tennis courts, swimming pools, and miniature golf. $$–$$$. (707) 279–4281.

**Best Western El Grande Inn.** 15135 Lakeshore Drive, Clearlake, CA 95422. A good-sized (seventy rooms) and relatively new motel near the lake, this Best Western offers convenience and economy. $$. (707) 994–2000.

**Anchorage Inn.** 950 Main Street, Lakeport, CA 95453. A smaller inn (thirty-five rooms) on the lake's northwest shore, this motel has been a standby for years, with a small swimming pool and lake access. Some rooms have kitchenettes. $$. (707) 263–5417.

## UKIAH

Continue west on CA-20 to the junction with US-101 (about 30 miles from Upper Lake) and go south about 10 miles to Ukiah, a bustling center of commerce in the sprawling Yokayo Valley. With its ancestry in the logging industry, Ukiah has long been the stomping ground of rednecks and roughnecks, and the town still has a gritty, all-American working-class feel to it. Also important to the town's culture are the nearby Yokayo Indians, whose rancherias finger into the valleys east of town. The last twenty years or so, Ukiah has been a hub for a new breed of Mendocino County farmers: marijuana growers, whose illegal plantations lie camouflaged throughout the nearby hillsides.

Like many small towns in northern California, Ukiah has also seen a recent influx of folks relocating from the crazier and pricier communities of the San Francisco Bay Area (Ukiah is about 120 miles from San Francisco). Along with them have come the Volvos, the gourmet-coffee shops, and the upscale restaurants, not to mention the scorn of longtime locals who rue the town's inevitable growth.

## WHERE TO GO

**Greater Ukiah Chamber of Commerce.** 200 South School Street, Ukiah, CA 95482. A quick stop here will set you up with information on Ukiah and much of Mendocino County. Lodging and dining information is available, as are maps to nearby wineries and recreation areas. (707) 462–4705.

**Grace Hudson Museum and Sun House.** 431 Main Street, Ukiah, CA 95482. More or less the pride of Ukiah, this complex celebrates the life and work of painter Grace Carpenter Hudson, who lived here from 1912 until her death in 1937. In addition to her paintings, the museum displays historical photos and her collection of basketry by Pomo Indians, whom Hudson often painted. Open Wednesday through Sunday; donations suggested. (707) 467–2836.

## WHERE TO STAY

**Vichy Springs Resort.** 2605 Vichy Springs Road, Ukiah, CA 95482. This rustic, low-key resort on 700 acres, the site of a naturally carbonated 90-degree hot springs, is a registered California Historical Landmark, having soothed weary travelers from Pomo Indians to Ulysses S. Grant and Jack London ("my favorite summer home," London wrote). In addition, there's an Olympic-size pool, and various massages and herbal treatments are available. Accommodations (some with kitchens) are available in the ranch-style main building or in separate cottages. $$–$$$. Day-use is about $35 per person. (707) 462–9515.

## BOONVILLE

From Ukiah continue south about 3 miles on Highway 101 to the junction of CA-253, a very narrow and winding road that takes you up into the heights of the Coast Range and drops you down into Boonville, a little community in the ripe apple- and grape-growing Anderson Valley.

"Boontling," the town's own "language," was invented in the early part of the twentieth century by locals with both a sense of humor and a desire to keep insular their little community. "Boontling" has been the subject of numerous newspaper and magazine articles over the years and was the Ph.D. dissertation topic of at least one linguist. Local boosters still like to point to Boontling as what sets it apart from other communities, although you'd be hard pressed to find someone who remembers much, if any, of it. Examples: "bucky walter" (pay phone), "shoveltooth" (doctor—apparently the town's first doctor had buck teeth), and "madge" (brothel, named for one of Ukiah's madams). The "language" was actually more of a separate vocabulary, probably not unlike the "languages" kids invent to talk about things adults think they're too young to talk about.

## WHERE TO EAT

**Anderson Valley Brewing Company and Buckhorn Saloon.** 14081 Highway 128, Boonville, CA 95415. I always try to plan my visits to this area so that I'm in Boonville around lunchtime. This brew pub (brewing some of the finest specialty beers this side of the Sierra Nevada Brewery) serves very good pub grub in an old-timey saloon-type restaurant. Burgers, salads, pasta dishes, fish, beef—all particularly tasty when washed down with an Anderson Valley ale, lager, or stout. $$-$$$. (707) 895-2337.

  **Boont Berry Farm.** 13981 Highway 128, Boonville, CA 95415. This little market specializes in locally grown organic produce and is one of the best places around to pick up picnic fixin's. $. (707) 895-3576.

## WHERE TO STAY

**Boonville Hotel.** 14050 Highway 128, Boonville, CA 95415. This small inn on the main drag in town was the site during the 1980s of one of the country's most famous and upscale restaurants, receiving rave reviews from well-known food critics throughout the culinary world. Unfortunately, its owners closed down shop one night, walked out the back door, and never came back, reportedly prompted by unpayable debts. Today lodging is available at the hotel, the restaurant has reopened under new ownership and management, and the place has bounced back quite gracefully. $$. (707) 895-2210.

# Regional Information

### DAY TRIP 1
Yuba-Sutter Chamber of Commerce
429 Tenth Street
Box 1429
Marysville, CA 95901
(530) 743-6501

### DAY TRIP 2
Sacramento National Wildlife Refuge
752 County Road 99W
Willows, CA 95988
(530) 934-2801

### DAY TRIP 3
Oroville Area Chamber of Commerce
1789 Montgomery Street
Oroville, CA 95965
(530) 538-2542 or (800) 655-4653

Paradise Ridge Visitor's Bureau
5550 Skyway
Box 1453
Paradise, CA 95967
(530) 877-9356

### DAY TRIP 4
Chico Chamber of Commerce and Visitors Bureau
330 Salem Street
Chico, CA 95928
(530) 891-5556 or (800) 852-8570

# NORTHEAST

## DAY TRIP 1

Grass Valley and Nevada County Chamber of Commerce
248 Mill Street
Grass Valley, CA 95945
(530) 273-4667 or (800) 655-4667

Nevada City Chamber of Commerce
132 Main Street
Nevada City, CA 95959
(530) 265-2692 or (800) 655-6569

## DAY TRIP 2

Truckee-Donner Chamber of Commerce
12036 Donner Pass Road
Truckee, CA 96161
(530) 587-2757

North Lake Tahoe Resort Association
245 North Lake Boulevard
Box 884
Tahoe City, CA 96145
(530) 581-6900

# EAST

## DAY TRIP 1

El Dorado County Chamber of Commerce
542 Main Street
Placerville, CA 95667
(530) 621-5885

## DAY TRIP 2

South Lake Tahoe Chamber of Commerce
3066 Lake Tahoe Boulevard
South Lake Tahoe, CA 96150
(530) 521-5255

## SOUTHEAST

**DAY TRIP 1**

Sutter Creek Visitor Information
40 Main Street
Box 600
Sutter Creek, CA 95685
(209) 267-1344

Amador County Chamber of Commerce
125 Peek Street
Jackson, CA 95642
(209) 223-0350

Calaveras County Visitors Center
1211 South Main
Angels Camp, CA 95222-0637
(209) 736-0049

## SOUTH

**DAY TRIP 1**

Rio Vista Chamber of Commerce
75 Main Street
Rio Vista, CA 95471
(707) 374-2700

## SOUTHWEST

**DAY TRIP 1**

Davis Chamber of Commerce
228 B Street
Davis, CA 95616
(530) 756-5160

## DAY TRIP 2

Vallejo Chamber of Commerce
2 Florida Street
Vallejo, CA 94590
(707) 644-5551

Benicia Chamber of Commerce
610 First Street
Benicia, CA 94510
(707) 745-2120 or (800) 559-7377

Berkeley Convention and Visitors Bureau
2015 Center Street
Berkeley, CA 94704
(510) 549-7040

Oakland Convention and Visitors Authority
550 Tenth Street, Suite 214
Oakland, CA 94607
(510) 839-9000 or (800) 262-5526

## DAY TRIP 3

San Francisco Convention and Visitor Bureau
Box 429097
San Francisco, CA 94142-9097
(415) 391-2000

## DAY TRIP 4

Sausalito Chamber of Commerce
333 Caledonia Street
Box 566
Sausalito, CA 94965
(415) 332-0505

# WEST

## DAY TRIP 1

Napa Conference and Visitors Bureau
1310 Napa Town Center
Napa, CA 94559
(707) 226-7459

Yountville Chamber of Commerce
6516 Yount Street
Yountville, CA 94599
(707) 944-0904

St. Helena Chamber of Commerce
1010 Main Street
Box 124
St. Helena, CA 94574
(707) 963-4456

Calistoga Chamber of Commerce
1458 Lincoln Street, #9
Calistoga, CA 94515
(707) 942-6333

## DAY TRIP 2

Sonoma Valley Visitors Bureau
453 First Street
Sonoma, CA 95476
(707) 996-1090

## DAY TRIP 3

Petaluma Visitor Program
799 Baywood Drive
Petaluma, CA 94954
(707) 769-0429

Sonoma County Visitors Bureau
2300 County Center Drive, Suite B260
Santa Rosa, CA 95403
(707) 565-2146

Sebastopol Chamber of Commerce
265 Main Street
Sebastopol, CA 95472
(707) 823-3032

Healdsburg Chamber of Commerce
217 Healdsburg Avenue
Healdsburg, CA 95448
(707) 433-6935

## NORTHWEST

### DAY TRIP 1

Lake County Visitors Information Center
875 Lakeport Drive
Lakeport, CA 95453
(707) 263-9544

Greater Ukiah Chamber of Commerce
200 South School Street
Ukiah, CA 95482
(707) 462-4705

# Festivals and Celebrations

**New Year's Day Swim,** San Francisco. Even if you don't have what it takes to jump into the icy bay to celebrate the new year, you might want to head on down to Aquatic Park and watch. Hosted by the Dolphin Swim and Boat Club, the annual event is a long-standing San Francisco tradition. (415) 391–2000.

**Sturgeon Derby,** Rio Vista. This two-day fishing competition focuses on the monster sturgeon that lurk in the delta's depths and are probably the best-tasting fish ever to grace a dinner plate. The derby is sponsored by the Trap Bait Shop in Rio Vista. (707) 374–2315.

**Mustard Festival,** Napa Valley. This monthlong celebration includes music festivals, art shows, wine and food tastings, special tours, a marathon, and a dance. January is actually one of the best times to visit the area, as there are far fewer people than in summer and fall (harvest season), and the vineyards claim a stark beauty: great expanses of pruned vines rolling in rigid rows over hillsides, with bright yellow mustard blossoms carpeting the ground between them. (707) 259–9020.

**San Francisco Chinese New Year,** San Francisco. It's easy to forget that not everybody celebrated the turn of the new millennium according to the Gregorian calendar. But for a reminder, check out Chinatown's new-year celebration. Whether it's the Year of the Dog, Snake, or Dragon, you'll see fireworks, parades, and stunning costumes. (415) 391–2000.

**Isleton Chinese New Year,** Isleton. Largely settled by Chinese in the late nineteenth and early twentieth centuries, Isleton celebrates the Chinese New Year delta style. There are rickshaw races, lion dancers, a parade, and fireworks. (916) 777–5880.

## MARCH

**Bidwell Classic,** Chico. The annual spring half-marathon through beautiful Bidwell Park also includes a 3-mile "fun-run" for the less competitive. (530) 345-1000.

**Home, Garden, and Antique Show,** Chico. Spread throughout several large buildings at the Silver Dollar Fairgrounds, this is just what you need for the winter doldrums. Get ideas for remodeling, replanting, and rejuvenating. (530) 899-4767.

**California State Old Time Fiddle Festival,** Oroville. Drawing musicians and fans from around the country, this is an increasingly popular event, held at the Municpal Auditorium. Attend the concerts or simply wander through the parking lot, where an impromptu jam on "Soldier's Joy" or "Blackberry Blossom" is likely to include fiddles, guitars, Dobros, stand-up basses, and banjos, played by gray-haired grandfathers and pony-tailed teens, the music bridging the generation gaps. (530) 538-2542.

**Celtic Fiddle Festival,** Chico. Featuring some of the best Scottish and Irish fiddlers in the world, this festival takes place on the campus of California State University, Chico. Tickets available for the show as well for the before-show traditional Irish dinner. (530) 898-5791.

**St. Patrick's Day Parade,** San Francisco. In a city whose residents take their national heritage rather seriously—and where a large number are of Irish descent—this is one of the biggest and craziest celebrations around. Pour yourself a Guinness or a shot of Tullamore Dew and join in the fun. (415) 391-2000.

## APRIL

**San Francisco International Film Festival.** Attracting well-known directors, producers, and actors, this festival features showings at theaters around the city, and though the focus is on new, independent films, there are also frequently retrospectives, as well as lectures and seminars. (415) 391-2000.

**Butter and Eggs Days Parade,** Petaluma. Not only a parade, games, and food booths, but a contest for the "Cutest Little Chick." Check out those drumsticks . . . (707) 762-9348.

**Gold Nugget Days,** Paradise. This celebration pays tribute to Paradise's gold-rush history, especially the huge gold nugget that marked the town's founding. There's a parade, crafts booths, and live music. Plus you can pan for gold (which has been planted in sluice boxes). (530) 872-8722.

**Apple Blossom Festival,** Sebastopol. Commemorating the apple's important contribution to the local economy, this celebration—first held in 1947—includes a parade, contests, and, of course, food booths. There are more things to do with an apple than you might realize. Located at Ives Park. (707) 823-3032.

## MAY

**Downtown Concert Series,** Chico. Each Friday evening at 7:00, through September, you can listen to free live music at the downtown plaza. Bring a lawn chair and a picnic dinner and tap your feet, whether it's Dixieland, blues, Celtic, rock 'n' roll, or bluegrass. (530) 345-6500.

**Cinco de Mayo,** San Francisco. The City's Mission District, largely Hispanic, pulls out all the stops, with a parade, lots of music, and food, the wonderful smells of carne adada wafting through the neighborhood. (415) 391-2000.

**Bay to Breakers,** San Francisco. Folks come from all over the world to take part in this wild, 7-mile footrace along the (closed off) streets of San Francisco, finishing up through Golden Gate Park and at the beach. Up to 100,000 participants, most in costume—some wearing nothing more than a pair of running shoes—get crazy as they sprint, walk, dance, and push strollers up and down hills. A highlight is the "centipede" costume category: Runners must be linked. Past winners have included buses, dragons, and everything else imaginable. Usually someone gets married en route. Oh, and some people take it seriously: The top-seeded runners are usually across the finish line before many have crossed the starting point. Afterwards, there's a free concert in the park. (415) 777-7770.

**Luther Burbank Rose Parade and Festival,** Santa Rosa. Celebrating Santa Rosa's famous horticulturist, this popular event includes live music, food booths, children's activities, and an antiques fair. Held in downtown Santa Rosa. (707) 542-7673.

**Mountain Play,** Marin County. This is one of the highlights of late spring-early summer in the Bay Area, an outdoor musical staged atop Mount Tamalpais with views of San Francisco and San Francisco Bay as a backdrop. Playgoers spread out blankets in the large stone amphitheater built as a 1930s WPA project and, in true Marin fashion, picnic on Brie, fresh San Francisco sourdough, and Chardonnay. (415) 388-9700.

**Calaveras County Fair and Jumping Frog Jubilee,** Angels Camp. Celebrating the amazing jumping frogs made famous in Mark Twain's short story, this is one of the highlights of events in the gold country, and one Angels Camp plays up for all it's worth. First held in 1928 to celebrate the paving of the main street through town, the celebration today gets national and international press, and contestants and their trainers come from all over the world. If you're frogless and want to join in, you can rent a frog for about $10. No guarantees. (209) 736-2561.

**Whole Earth Festival,** Davis (UC Davis campus). Weekend-long event to promote holistic living, recycling, and other earth-friendly pursuits. Live music, dancing, poetry, seminars, and lots of tie-dye, flowers, and braids. (530) 752-1011.

## JUNE

**San Francisco Lesbian, Gay, Bisexual, and Transgender Pride Celebration Parade,** San Francisco (where else!). One of the wildest parties in town, this anything-goes celebration attracts thousands of participants, including the notorious Dikes on Bikes, and gawkers. The parade's serious side (acknowledging individuality and refuting intolerance) helps instill honor and pride in the community. (415) 864-3733.

**Bloomsday,** Chico. Celebrating James Joyce's masterpiece, *Ulysses* (on June 16, the day the action in the novel takes place), this festival includes music, poetry, readings from Joyce, and stage adaptations of Joyce's work. Though local professors contribute to the evening's festivities, the celebration is decidedly, and intentionally, unacademic. Attendees need not be Joyce scholars, or even have read the book, though a love of language and a sense of humor are prerequisites. In recent years Chico's Bloomsday has been listed in *The Irish Times* as one of the best in the world, along with those in Dublin, Sydney, New York City, and Boston. Guinness is served on tap. (530) 895-3749.

**Plaza Art and Artisan Show,** Sonoma. For nearly four decades, this show, sponsored by the Valley of the Moon Art Association, has featured a wide array of quality arts and crafts from Sonoma-area artists. Located on the Sonoma Plaza. (707) 996-2115.

**Music in the Mountains,** Grass Valley and Nevada City. This annual three-week concert series features a variety of classical music played in various venues throughout the area. (530) 265-6124.

**Crawdad Festival,** Isleton. This huge three-day festival—one of the biggest on the delta—attracts as many as 200,000 participants, who delight in crawdad cooked every way imaginable (and some unimaginable). Plus there's live music (twenty bands) and arts and crafts. (916) 777-5880.

## JULY

**Fourth of July,** Chico. Chico's Western League Baseball Team, the Heat, put on a wonderful fireworks display over the stadium. Best viewed from inside the stadium, but you can see from the surrounding neighborhoods as well. (530) 343-4328.

**Fourth of July,** Truckee. Classic small-town Independence Day celebration, with a parade, live music, crafts, and food. Bonus: the mild daytime temperatures and cool nights, particularly compared with Sacramento-area temperatures on the Fourth of July. (530) 587-2757.

**Oroville Blues and Culture Festival,** Oroville. Held at Martin Luther King, Jr., Park, this annual festival attracts big-name blues players and includes music and crafts fairs. (530) 538-2542.

**Marin County Fair,** San Rafael. A traditional county fair with definite new-agey, West-Coast flavor. Get a massage after your Ferris-wheel ride; wash your tofu-dog down with bottled springwater. (415) 454-4163 or (800) 454-4163.

**California Trail Days,** Truckee. This fair, held at Donner Memorial State Park, celebrates the hardy pioneers (not only the Donners) who came west in the nineteenth century. The festival includes a parade and historical reenactments, with authentic costumes, wagons, and other artifacts of the Old West. (530) 582-7892.

**Pear Fair,** Courtland. Celebrating the area's main industry, this event includes a parade, recipe contests, and a huge range of pear-based food and drink. (916) 775-2000.

## AUGUST

**Dipsea Footrace,** Mill Valley. This grueling race over Mount Tamalpais and down to the ocean has nearly a century of history and attracts runners from around the country. Unlike the Bay to Breakers, this is not a frivolous affair and should be undertaken by in-shape runners only. (415) 388-9700.

**International Stand-up Comedy Competition,** San Francisco. Many winners of this highly acclaimed festival—viewed as a stepping stone for comics on their way up—have gone on to great success, on television and in film. An elimination-type tournament, the final round pits the last two competitors against each other in a no-holds-barred laugh-off. (415) 391-2000.

**Truckee Championship Rodeo,** Truckee. Come on out and see bronc riders, dogie ropers, and the classic rodeo clowns. There's also a barbecue and western dance. (530) 582-9852.

**Yuba-Sutter Fair,** Yuba City. A classic American regional fair, with live-stock shows, rides, live music, a demolition derby, and a beauty pageant. Held at the Yuba-Sutter Fairgrounds. (530) 674–1280.

**Zucchini Festival,** Healdsburg. In honor of the lowly zucchini, often home-grown and typically foisted by armloads on neighbors this time of the year, this celebration includes competition for best recipes, biggest zucchini, and "zucchini-car" races. (707) 431–1956.

# SEPTEMBER

**Celtic Festival,** Sebastopol. Three days of Celtic music and culture—concerts, music workshops, films, crafts booths, and food. A great opportunity to hear some of the best fiddlers and folk groups working the Celtic-music circuit, as well as a chance to pick up some new licks yourself and to learn more about how the Irish saved civilization. Each year this festival attracts bigger-name musicians and a larger audience, yet its rural setting provides for a much mellower pace than that at the Celtic Festival in San Francisco. (707) 823–3032.

**Renaissance Festival,** Vacaville. This five-weekend-long fair celebrates the bawdy eclectic. Put on your leggings or best Renaissance dress and come join the fun. Toss overripe tomatoes at the poor fellow in stocks; watch knights do battle on horseback; listen to traveling minstrels sing songs of olde; wash a turkey drumstick down with a glass of mead or ale; fire a crossbow; watch randy wenches make light of poor peasants. A guaranteed good tyme. (707) 453–0153.

**Chico World Music Festival,** Chico. This festival has been gathering steam in the ten years or so of its existence, each year attracting more and better-known musicians, from Celtic to African to South American. Held either inside at Laxson Auditorium on the California State University, Chico campus or outside in Bidwell Park. (530) 891–4081.

**Valley of the Moon Vintage Festival,** Sonoma. Located on the downtown plaza, this event, the oldest wine celebration in the state, includes a parade, food, music, and a general giving-of-thanks to the great (fermented) grape. (707) 996–2109.

**Wheelchair Tennis Tournament,** Truckee. Attracting the best tennis players in wheelchairs from around the world, this event is sponsored by the United States Tennis Association and has been held in Truckee since 1985. (530) 587–2108.

# OCTOBER

**Sonoma County Fair,** Santa Rosa. Everything one loves and hates about a county fair, from corndogs and eggrolls-on-a-stick to Ferris-wheel rides and livestock shows. Win a 4-foot-tall stuffed roadrunner by knocking down the lead milk bottles with the sawdust softball. (707) 528-3247.

**Book Farm Harvest Festival,** Chico. As a benefit for local organizations, this farm between Chico and Oroville invites the public to take part in a scarecrow contest, hayrides, and pancake breakfast. In addition, you can buy pumpkins ranging from Ping-Pong-ball-size to just smaller than Volkswagens. (530) 893-3139.

**Columbus Day Parade,** San Francisco. Though attacked by some people as being insensitive to cultures taken advantage of by European conquest, this century-old parade still brings out the revelers, thanks in part to its location in North Beach, where a large portion of the residents are of Italian descent. (415) 391-2000.

**Fleet Week,** San Francisco. Highlights here include public tours of U.S. Navy ships, overhead demonstrations by the Blue Angels, and simply the spectacle of the monstrous watercraft sailing underneath the Golden Gate Bridge, their decks lined with saluting sailors. (415) 391-2000.

**Rio Vista Bass Derby,** Rio Vista. Begun in the middle of the last century, this is one of the oldest fishing tournaments in the state. In addition to fishing for prize bass, you can view a parade, listen to live music, check out a car show, and sample lots of food at a wide range of booths. (707) 374-2700.

**Salmon Festival,** Oroville. Celebrating the huge fall run of salmon in the nearby Feather and Sacramento Rivers, this festival stresses local Native American culture and includes arts and crafts, food, and children's activities, as well as fishing demonstrations. (530) 533-2011.

**World's Arm-Wrestling Championships**, Petaluma. This has been a Petaluma tradition for decades and has even been featured on ESPN. Unlike any other competition, this tournament attracts biceps from around the country. (707) 762-9348.

## NOVEMBER

**Christmas Preview,** Chico. Check out the retail shops of downtown Chico, many of which serve cider and cookies and have live entertainment in their display windows and on showroom floors, from mimes to Nutcracker ballerinas to harpists. You can also hop aboard the haywagon, for a horse-drawn tour of downtown, and Santa will add your name to his list. (530) 345-6500.

**Christmas at Bidwell Mansion State Historic Park, Open House,** Chico. Tour this nineteenth-century Italian-villa-style home of Chico founders John and Annie Bidwell when it's decorated in all its Victorian-era Christmas finery. (530) 895-6144.

**Sikh Parade,** Yuba City. One of the largest Sikh parades in North America, put on by the Sikh community that is heavily involved in agriculture in the area. Food booths, music, crafts. (530) 743-6501.

## DECEMBER

**Crab season,** San Francisco. Traditionally beginning on December 1, but having been pushed back in recent years, crab season in San Francisco is celebrated throughout the city, but particularly at Fisherman's Wharf. The Dungeness crabs cook in boilers on sidewalks, and you can pick them up for sometimes as little as $2.00 a pound. Best washed down with a locally brewed Anchor Steam beer. (415) 391-2000.

**Heritage Homes Christmas Parlour Tour,** Petaluma. Many of Petaluma's gorgeously restored Victorian homes are decorated for the holidays and open to the public for tours. (707) 762-3456.

**Dickens Fair,** San Francisco. This annual festival celebrates nineteenth-century England with a crafts fair (aimed, obviously, at Christmas shoppers). Lots of food, spirits, and live music. (415) 391-2000.

**Christmas at the Sonoma Mission,** Sonoma. An old-world-style welcoming of Christmas, including caroling, a candlelight procession, and nondenominational church services. There's cider and hot chocolate for participants. (707) 938-1519.

**Rio Vista Lighted Boat Christmas Parade,** Rio Vista. This is a parade of boats, their decks and masts decorated with strings of Christmas lights. The parade route is the Delta Marina to the Rio Vista Bridge. (707) 374-2700.

**Nevada City Christmas,** Nevada City. Recently listed in *Sunset* magazine as one of the best towns for Christmas lights and decorations in the West, Nevada City dresses its citizens and downtown buildings in Victorian garb and celebrates the season in grand style. (530) 265-2692.

# Parks and Recreation Areas

California State Parks are scattered up and down the state, from the Mexico border north to Oregon and from the Pacific Ocean east to Nevada. Some of the best of them are within short drives of Sacramento and would make for great trips themselves, or for overnight camping. The state-park system has been divided into districts, and at least parts of five of them are within two hours of Sacramento: the Gold Country, the North Coast, the Central Valley, the High Sierra, and the San Francisco Bay Area. In the High Sierra district, for example, you can visit Lake Tahoe's D. L. Bliss, Emerald Bay, and Sugarpine Point state parks, all of which offer swimming, camping, fishing, picnicking, hiking, and hot showers. In the Central Valley, on the other hand, state parks offer everything from bird-watching to historical tours. At Bidwell Mansion State Historic Park, you can learn about the life of two of California's most intriguing pioneers and tour their nineteenth-century Italianate home. In the San Francisco Bay Area district, you can hike, mountain bike, and take in stunning vistas of San Francisco Bay from Mount Tamalpais State Park.

And this is just the tip of the iceberg. For complete information on California State Parks, write California Department of Parks and Recreation, Box 942896, Sacramento, CA 94296-0001. You can also call (916) 653-6995. You can also learn about the parks, as well as make reservations for camping, at their Web site, cal-parks.ca.gov/.

Additionally, the state is home to several national recreation areas. Most notable is Golden Gate National Recreation Area at the north end of San Francisco and the south tip of Marin County, just across the Golden Gate Bridge. This gorgeous piece of property offers hiking, cycling, authentic bits of history, and views of the city, the bay, the Golden Gate Bridge, sometimes migrating gray whales, and, on clear days, the Farallon Islands, 27 miles offshore. For information on the Golden Gate National Recreation Area, call (415) 556-5801.

For information on hunting and fishing in California, contact the California Department of Fish and Game at (916) 653-7664.

# Guide to California Cuisine

First of all, a clarification: Of course, there is a "California cuisine," but what I want to talk about is the huge variety of kinds of food you're likely to find in your travels in California, from little mom-and-pop Mexican taquerias in San Francisco's Mission District and the Sacramento Valley to the upscale, white-linen, nationally acclaimed restaurants of the Bay Area and the wine country, where you're quite likely to come face to plate with some definitive "California cuisine."

The simple reason that there are so many kinds of food in California is that the state's population is so diverse. First colonized by the Spanish in the late eighteenth and early nineteenth centuries, and in the twentieth and twenty-first centuries a destination for hundreds of thousands of migrant Mexican farmworkers, the state has a palpable Hispanic feel to it. That makes for lots of good Mexican food and excellent Mexican restaurants. In addition to tacos you'll find burritos, chile rellenos, enchiladas, and other classics, as well as more contemporary dishes focusing on natural, home-grown ingredients. Some indications that a Mexican restaurant is authentic: (1) The sign on the door says *abierto* (Spanish for "open"); (2) you shouldn't have to spend more than $8.00 for dinner; (3) there's likely to be a small, black-and-white television in the kitchen—or even the lobby or dining room—tuned to a Spanish-language station; and (4) the breakfast menu includes menudo (tripe, said to be the ultimate hangover cure).

California was also settled by large numbers of Italian immigrants, some of whom came in the great Gold Rush of 1849 and .who started families and opened businesses. Some businesses are presently run by Italian families who can trace their roots back five, six, and more generations. And some of those businesses are restaurants. Of course, many of those restaurants are in San Francisco, particularly in the North Beach area, where many Italians settled.

But there are also exceptional Italian restaurants in western Marin and Sonoma Counties, where Italians have run farms and ranches since the late nineteenth century, and also in the gold country, where many miners stayed after the gold played out. The best of these restaurants are unpretentious, family-style places, where the noise level is often high and chianti flows freely. Among the best things the Italians have bestowed on California: lasagna, cioppino (with fresh seafood), and pasta dishes with marinara and clam sauces.

Many other immigrants have left indelible marks on California cooking. And while Chinese restaurants have existed throughout California, today, even outside the urban areas, you're likely to run across Japanese, Thai, Vietnamese, Greek, Indian, and even North African restaurants.

Another very popular type of California restaurant is the brew pub. Relative newcomers to the California dining scene—having first appeared in the mid-1980s—brew pubs are generally moderately priced and dependably good restaurants, defined by the fact that they brew their own beers and ales, which are also often used in their cooking. Main dishes usually include fish and chips, sausages, burgers, salads, pastas, soups, and sandwiches, as well as grilled meats and seafood.

The flagship of the brew-pub fleet is Sierra Nevada Brewery in Chico, which has grown from one of the most respected microbreweries in the United States to the tenth-largest brewery in the country, outgrowing its microbrewery status. Recently remodeled and expanded, and known for its rocking tap parties (when a new seasonal beer is launched), Sierra Nevada alone is worth a day trip (be sure to designate a driver).

California is also one of the great places in the world for seafood, particularly San Francisco, where crab, sea bass, calamari, and other fish is served virtually right off the boat. A good seafood restaurant, such as the Pacific Cafe in San Francisco, will typically feature up to a dozen different seafood dishes on its menu, plus several "catches of the day." These can include swordfish, ahi, salmon, and sturgeon, not to mention abalone, the *crème de la crème* of seafood. Usually, seafood dishes are served with a small salad, perhaps a side of pilaf, and a serving of fresh vegetables.

So what about "California cuisine"?

Generally, restaurants that advertise California cuisine pride themselves on fresh (often organically grown) local ingredients, sometimes grown in on-the-premises herb and vegetable gardens. Local meats are used when available, though the focus of the restaurants is rarely meat, and certainly not the big slabs of beef you'd find at a steakhouse. Instead, look for lamb, fowl, and small pieces of high-end cuts of beef. Many of the entrees reflect a continental influence, particularly French.

Restaurants specializing in California cuisine also typically pride themselves on their entrees' "presentation," which is much more important than size of serving. Your tiny cup of corn-and-garlic soup might be topped with a swath of currant sauce or garnished with a sprig of mint or a circlet of grape leaves. Your salmon fillet might be dressed in herbed butter and shallots and served beside a small portion of risotto. Your squab might be garnished with sage, your fettuccini with mustard greens and olives.

The other thing that typifies California cuisine is price. Though the food is always good, and always fresh, it's almost always expensive. Lunches run $8.00 to $12.00, and dinners $10.00 to $25.00. Often the entrees are a la carte, so if you have a soup or salad to go with, you'll be paying even more.

Chez Panisse in Berkeley was the pioneer of California cuisine back in the early 1970s and still sets the standard by which all the others are judged. Chef-owner Alice Waters has become a celebrity in the cooking world, having consulted on numerous other restaurants, taught cooking classes, and authored cookbooks.

*A final word:* Keep in mind that most waitpersons are working for less than the minimum wage and rely on tips to make a decent living. Plan to tip at least 15 percent, and for particularly good service, as much as 20 percent or more. They work hard and deserve it.

# ABOUT THE AUTHOR

Stephen Metzger has spent much of the last forty years taking the day trips discussed in this book. Born in San Francisco and raised in Marin County, he traveled extensively throughout the northern part of the state with his family, camping, fishing, hunting, until he moved to Colorado after graduating high school. After returning to Marin and then living in South Lake Tahoe for two years, he moved to Chico, where he became fascinated with the Sacramento Valley, exploring its every nook and cranny, yet continuing to take trips to the coast and the Sierras.

Stephen has written four other guidebooks, including *New Mexico Handbook* and *Colorado Handbook* (Moon Travel Handbooks). He has also written scores of essays and articles for national and international magazines and newspapers, including pieces for *Powder,* *Skiing,* the San Francisco *Examiner,* the San Francisco *Chronicle, AlaskaAirlines Magazine,* and many other travel, in-flight, and health-and-fitness publications. He also is a regular contributor to the *Chico News and Review,* and teaches in the English department at California State University, Chico.